Praise for
Change Your Questions, Change Your Future

This book is about change, which is something a lot of people are looking for in their lives. The best way to change your life is to change the way you talk to yourself. These questions and this way of thinking help you do that. There's a lot of clarity in these pages that will make your path forward seem like it was obvious the whole time.

— **Charlamagne Tha God**, *New York Times* best-selling author, host of *The Breakfast Club*, and founder and CEO of iHeartRadio's Black Effect Podcast Network

I wish I could have read these words at multiple low points throughout my life. Change Your Questions, Change Your Future *really takes me deeper into my purpose and how to align my life with that purpose. This book is for anyone who needs to know themselves better, so they can start to live up to their potential.*

— **Tiffany Haddish**, award-winning actress, comedian, and author

Also by Adam S. Froerer and Elliott E. Connie

Books

*The Solution Focused Brief Therapy Diamond: A New Approach to SFBT That Will Empower Both Practitioner and Client to Achieve the Best Outcomes**

Solution-Focused Brief Therapy with Clients Managing Trauma, with editors Jacqui von Cziffra-Bergs and Johnny Kim

Also by Elliott E. Connie

Books

The Art of Solution Focused Therapy, with editor Linda Metcalf

The Solution Focused Marriage: 5 Simple Habits That Will Bring Out the Best in Your Relationship

Solution Building in Couples Therapy

*Available from Hay House

Please visit:

Hay House India: www.hayhouse.co.in
Hay House USA: www.hayhouse.com®
Hay House Australia: www.hayhouse.com.au
Hay House UK: www.hayhouse.co.uk

Change Your Questions, Change Your Future

Change Your Questions, Change Your Future

Learn to Shift Your Perspective, Overcome Obstacles, and Create Lasting Change —One Question at a Time

ELLIOTT E. CONNIE, MA, LPC
ADAM S. FROERER, PhD, LMFT

HAY HOUSE INDIA
New Delhi • London • Sydney
Carlsbad, California • New York City

Hay House Publishers (India) Pvt Ltd
Muskaan Complex, Plot No. 3, B-2, Vasant Kunj, New Delhi - 110070, India

Hay House LLC, P.O. Box 5100, Carlsbad, CA 92018-5100, USA
Hay House UK Ltd, 1st Floor, Crawford Corner, 91-93 Baker Street, London W1U 6QQ, UK
Hay House Australia Publishing Pty Ltd, 18/36 Ralph St., Alexandria NSW 2015, Australia

Email: contact@hayhouse.co.in
Website: www.hayhouse.co.in

Project editor: Melody Guy
Indexer: Beverlee Day
Cover design: theBookDesigners
Interior design: Lilly Penhall

First published by Hay House India, 2026
Reprint, 2026
11 10 9 8 7 6 5 4 3 2

ISBN 978-93-6611-114-8

Printed at Repro India Limited

FSC www.fsc.org MIX Paper from responsible sources FSC® C047271

Hay House is committed to a sustainable future for our business, our readers and our planet. This book is made from Forest Stewardship Council® certified paper.

What outcome do you want from reading this book?

What difference would it make if you could attain it?

How would you notice the change it made in your life?

CONTENTS

INTRODUCTION

Let's start with a question: How do you become the very best version of yourself? The answer to this will transform your life and is the core of this book. The answer may surprise you because it's not about an answer at all. It's actually about learning to ask yourself better questions. Most people ask themselves the wrong questions and end up stuck in the same situation over and over again. However, those that master the art of asking themselves the kinds of questions that move them toward their goals become the very best version of themselves. That's what this book is about, and by the end of this text, you will be a master of this art and thus transformed into the very best version of you.

We (Elliott and Adam) are best friends who have mastered the art of asking questions. We are world-renowned psychotherapists who practice something called Solution Focused Brief Therapy. This kind of therapy is all about asking questions that move people toward their best selves. Solution focused questions have decades of research supporting their efficacy. We have dedicated ourselves to this work, and this book is an extension to what we have been doing clinically for over 40 years combined. In essence, reading this book will be as if you have seen us within our practices and will have a massive impact on your life.

Each chapter in this book is structured in an atypical manner. We are quite different from one another and often have very different perspectives and styles when it comes to explaining solution focused thought. To capture our individual styles and voices, we have included smaller sections within each chapter that are entitled "Diving Deep with Elliott" and "A Closer Look with Adam." These sections aren't meant to be contradictory or confusing but are meant to show that we can have different but complementary perspectives that, when woven together, make our appreciation for the approach even richer. We hope that you will consider both perspectives equally, and that they enhance your own understanding of solution focused questions and allow you to apply these questions to your life effectively. This book goes beyond just teaching you a list of questions. Instead, we will share the thinking behind these questions so that you can apply them to address your current life situations and any other obstacles that happen in your future.

In Part I of the book, we share our own stories, including stories of our friendship. These stories highlight experiences that have taught us a perspective that is very much in alignment with how we teach and practice SFBT, but more importantly, these experiences that have taught us the importance of working from a place of love and respect. We also highlight how overcoming discrimination and other challenges have paved the way for conceptualizing the solution focused approach in this unique and evolved way. Furthermore, these stories will help you get to know us better as individuals as you continue to read the book from our alternating voices and perspectives.

This gets to the second mission we have for this book. We want to help you become your best self, and we have this crazy and ambitious wish to make this world a better place. We're sticking with this aim. We share our story of an unlikely friendship and how two people from two different worlds built a bond based on love and use that bond to change the world.

By the end of this book, we hope that you walk away feeling inspired. We hope this book increases your ability to view yourself as strong, capable, and resilient. Most importantly, we hope you feel the love that we intended to pass to you through these pages. We hope this book inspires you to be the agent of change in your own life, to bring about your desired transformations, and become the version of yourself that you most want to be.

Many self-help books are about problems: if you have xyz problems, then read this book and get solutions to those specific problems. However, this book will be a very different experience. Just like the solution focused approach itself, this book is not problem specific. The questions we will teach you in this book, along with the thinking behind them, are designed to help you to become the best version of yourself and accomplish your biggest dreams. It doesn't matter what problems are bothering you currently or in the future. Mastering this skill will allow you to overcome those challenges and transform your life. So, here's what you won't find in this book: problem-solving language. Instead, you will get inspiring questions that will provide you with solutions to any problem that is troubling you as well as a few worksheets to allow you to put these questions to use in your life. This is how Solution Focused Brief Therapy works, and that's the foundation of this book. It's a different way of thinking, but it's how change and success happen. So, trust the process and get ready for massive transformation. It's all within the following pages.

Before we get started, one last thing: thank you for trusting us to be a small part of your life as we attempt to touch your heart and transform your life through the pages of this book. Enjoy!

PART I

An Introduction to Solution Focused Questioning

CHAPTER 1

ELLIOTT'S STORY

The first memory I have of my father is of him bathing me gently and holding me up in front of a mirror while drying me off. I thought he was the most awesome dad in the world, and I wanted to be just like him.

On Saturday mornings, we ate breakfast at the same time. He'd sit down to eat a bowl of cereal, and he'd hold the bowl in his left hand and the spoon in his right. I tried to hold my own bowl similarly, but I struggled with my little two-and-a-half-year-old hands. It wasn't long before I dropped the bowl and spilled the cereal. As a punishment, my father spanked me aggressively, even though I was only a toddler.

These two events—being bathed lovingly and spanked roughly—happened in close proximity. It should come as no surprise then to learn that my life as a child was filled with lies, fear, and anxiety. It was also a life spent trying to please my father . . . or in the very least trying not to upset him.

He was violent with everyone in my family—my two brothers, Mom, and me. I didn't feel like I could protect any of us from him, especially my mom. When I was 10 years old, my parents had a terrible fight, and my mother tried to defend herself by attempting to bite off his finger. He had to bandage it for a long time afterward because it was so gouged.

That event caused my self-esteem to decline even further because I didn't know how to keep my mother safe from my father, even though logically I knew that wasn't my responsibility.

Around that same time, when we were living in Boston after moving from Chicago, my father left my mother for the first time. Until then, we had been a middle-class family, but afterward we became a very low-income family. My mother raised my brothers and me on only $17,000 a year. My dad came and went, but he was always around, especially on the weekends—which was when the violence continued to happen.

When I was 19 years old, my mom had a nervous breakdown that resulted in us moving to Texas to live closer to her sister and farther away from my father. In his physical absence, my life started to get better, but when he saw proof of that improvement during his infrequent visits, he'd try to pull me down to feeling miserable again. I couldn't escape him.

When he was gone, he'd try to parent me over the phone, and his methods were aggressive, controlling, and outright mean. Despite that, I still sought his approval, and my life revolved around obtaining it.

Before we moved, I'd attended college at the University of Massachusetts–Dartmouth, but in Texas I had to restart my freshman year all over again. I felt horrible about myself. I had no money or resources. Not only was I starting over again, I was doing so in worse financial circumstances.

That was the darkest year of my life. I spent most of it not just contemplating but also accepting that I was going to commit suicide. Life as I knew it was not worth living, I told myself, so I wanted out.

I didn't feel sad. People often associate suicidality with sadness or even depression, but I believe it's associated with hopelessness, which was the case for me.

Colleges are difficult places to be when you're poor and different. I'd watch my peers walk to the mailbox to get gifts from their family, be it food, clothes, a computer, or money. Meanwhile, I had nothing.

The best way I can describe how I felt is I had no hope that my father's abuse and its repercussions were ever going to stop. I could see them extending throughout the rest of my life.

If this is life, I thought, *I don't want one.*

Everybody else seemed to get a better one than me.

One day I was lying in my dorm room, having fully accepted that as soon as I got the courage I was going to take my life.

It was then I had an epiphany: if I died, everyone was going to think something was wrong with me. My eulogy would be "Elliott was sad. Elliott was depressed."

But that wasn't my issue—my father's abuse was the reason I'd been pushed to this point—and somehow, I couldn't tolerate the thought of dying if that untruth would spread about me.

I wouldn't have minded if people said, "Elliott died because he got an unfair shake at life," but I didn't want them thinking I died because I had personal issues.

So there I was in my dorm room when I realized that dying because of my father's problems was unacceptable. I couldn't do it. And if dying for his problems was unacceptable, then I needed to discover how to live for myself.

Immediately, I changed the way I lived my life. I started by setting boundaries with my father. I gave him three rules: he couldn't yell at me, he couldn't call me names, and he couldn't hit me. "If you can do those three things," I said, "I'm quite happy to have a relationship with you."

We never spoke again. He wasn't willing to follow my rules.

Even though that year was the hardest one of my life, it was also the most satisfying. It was the year I learned I could protect myself emotionally. It was the year I learned that if I could stand up to my dad, I could accomplish absolutely anything.

I became utterly fearless. I became more faithful and spiritual. Above all, I became a man who could slay a dragon. I took control of my life. I knew hard days might come again in the future, but I was empowered with the knowledge that I'd already defeated the biggest and scariest dragon. Every other dragon would never be as threatening.

That day in my dorm room, I decided to go on an adventure, and it was an adventure of discovery. I knew what life had been like when I spent all of it trying to please my father. What I didn't know is what life could be like if I lived authentically as Elliott Connie.

My internal self-talk transformed. For the first time I began trying to achieve personal pride and satisfaction. I'd failed at trying to be who my dad wanted me to be, and I learned I could handle that failure. I might as well try to be who I was supposed to be.

And if I failed at that, so what? At least I'd fail while being true to myself. That new outlook was incredibly freeing.

The next semester, I worked out regularly and lost 50 pounds. I met my wife. I got a 4.0 GPA. I switched my major from marine biology to psychology because I was interested in the brain. I knew my father would say, "You can't make any money in psychology. What are you going to do with that degree?" But I didn't care. I started making decisions based on what felt right to me, and on that basis alone.

I no longer think about challenges in terms of being challenges. I've learned that I can endure anything. I'm used to reaching milestones that should have been simple but instead were very difficult. Because of that, difficulty doesn't make any difference to me.

I've developed a "Roger that" mentality. If I have to race someone around the block, and the other person gets a bike while I have to run, I say, "Roger that." I don't care what advantage anyone else has. My philosophy is that if I've got to do life hard, I'll do it hard. And when I accomplish what I set out to achieve, I want people to know that I didn't ask for any favors. Despite the obstacles in my path, I crossed the finish line and won.

Looking back on the early years of my life, I'm grateful for the pain and suffering I had to live with because it made me a good psychotherapist. I empathize with my clients. I practice an approach that enables change without causing further suffering.

One of the hallmarks of solution focused thought is that change doesn't have to take forever. I know because I lived it. In a dorm room, in just a moment, I changed my life.

Change can happen instantaneously.

SHIFTING YOUR PERSPECTIVE

Change Can Happen in an Instant

Diving Deep with Elliott

We're going to share concepts in this book that you may have a hard time digesting because they go against the reality that people have unintentionally bought into, which is that change takes a long time. It doesn't. Change can happen in an instant, as I learned for myself through the story I just shared.

You've also experienced a rapid change. How many of you have had a phone call, a text message, or an e-mail that changed your life, good or bad? I would venture to say all of you. Perhaps you got an e-mail that said, "Congratulations, you got the job!" Perhaps you got a phone call when you were told a loved one passed away. Each of you has experienced change in an instant.

Change can be apparent to others right away, or change can appear to be subtler. Adam's son, Toby, is now a high-achieving student, and that started when I had a conversation with him several months ago. Leading up to that conversation, I sent Adam a picture of me with Awkwafina when I met her. I asked Adam to show it to Toby because I knew he'd love it. In fact, I'd taken the picture with Toby in mind.

When I talked with Toby afterward, he was shocked and asked, "How did you meet Awkwafina?"

Knowing that Toby has always wanted to go to Los Angeles with me, and wanting to motivate him with his grades, I replied, "I'm meeting everyone every time I go to LA. I'll bring you with me, but you've got to get straight A's."

In that moment, Toby became a straight-A student. Did he actually have the straight-A report card yet? No. But the second he bought into the idea that he was a straight-A student, he was on the pathway to earning straight A's. And he's been getting better grades ever since. He is learning to manage dyslexia (which he discovered he has after the deal was made) and learning to do so with the belief that he can be a straight-A student.

Sometimes life takes a while to offer the evidence, but change can happen in an instant.

RETRAINING YOUR BRAIN ABOUT CHANGE

A Closer Look with Adam

Sometimes people have the perspective that, while change is clearly happening, it's beyond our control. For instance, we know we're always getting older. We're either speeding up or slowing down. If we deal with illness, we're either feeling better or worse.

But what you *can* change is your perspective of change and by doing so take control of the way you interact with change. In some sense, you can manipulate change.

While change happens in different ways, it's always happening. You can alter your perspective of it, how much you interact with it, and your trajectory of it. You can instantly change who you are.

There are people who suddenly stop smoking or drinking and never go back. They said, "I'm going to do something different." Their environment didn't change, the people they associate with didn't change, but their perspective of their control over their addiction changed.

When my son, Toby, had that conversation with Elliott about becoming a straight-A student so he could go to LA, his perspective changed. Now he thought change was possible. He hadn't demonstrated proof of that change yet, but he thought, *Okay, I'm going to do things differently to achieve what I want.*

For another person, perhaps the proof comes first. Let's say she's a runner who just happened to have a good day and suddenly broke a record. But that instance isn't what really changed her. She must have been training for a long time. And even though the moment wasn't happenstance after all, it was still the moment she realized, "I did it. And I can keep doing it." That moment still served as a pivotal moment of change for her.

CHANGING YOUR RELATIONSHIP WITH YOUR "PROBLEM"

Diving Deep with Elliott

While I was growing up, my family and I were churchgoers, and in the Black community, that meant church was a very large part of our lives. It was the center of our community, even our neighborhood in Boston. I not only attended church on Sundays, but also went to youth group and Bible study as well as other church events on most days of the week. On some level, my family and I interacted with people in our church every day.

When I was 10 years old, our church decided to go on a field trip to New York City. The leadership of a congregation there chartered a bus to drive some of our congregation to New York City. As a member of whatever committee in our local church at the time, my mom was eligible to attend the field trip and bring me with her.

Now, this trip coincided with the time in my life that I first started having suicidal thoughts, which were very dark thoughts to be alone with on a long bus ride with none of the distractions kids these days have with their iPads and iPhones.

We began the trip around 2:00 in the morning, and the bus driver said we would arrive in New York City around 8 A.M. I was deep in the trenches of my horrible thoughts when I heard a huge *boom* that shook our bus.

The driver pulled off to the side of the road, then got out and milled around for bit, investigating what had caused the bus to break down. He soon came back and announced that we had a flat tire. Another bus was on its way to help change the tire, and then we could continue our journey.

We sat on the bus for what felt like forever, waiting for the other bus to arrive. When lots of time passed, and it hadn't come yet, the bus driver did some more investigating outside. Soon he made a new announcement: "It's actually not a flat tire; it's a broken axle." This required a whole different bus to come and help us. But by the time that bus finally came and fixed it, it was too late for us to go on to New York City. We had to turn around and return to Boston.

As you can imagine, I felt devastated at not being able to complete the trip. On top of that, I was also confused. "Mom, this was a bus of churchgoing people going to do a church thing," I said. "If there was a single vehicle on the road that should have had God's protection, wouldn't it have been this bus?"

Now, being a very wise woman, my mom sensed what I was actually asking: Why do bad things happen to good people?

I'll never forget how she put her hand on my leg and replied, "Sometimes God puts you through hard things to prepare you for something later in life."

In that profound moment, my mom changed my relationship to the problem. I thought about her words for the rest of the way home, a three-hour drive, as we'd broken down halfway between New York and Boston.

As I kept pondering, I concluded that what she said must mean one of two things: I was either living a really difficult childhood to prepare me for a really difficult adulthood, or I was living it to prepare me to do something amazing.

Looking back, I recognize now what a brilliant shift of mind that was for my young 10-year-old self. It was also when I began to be hopeful. *Maybe I'm having muscles built,* I thought, *like mental muscles so I can do something hard. And I hope it's something good.*

I still struggled with suicidal thoughts. I still struggled with sadness. But I became much more resilient from that point forward because I wanted to see what adulthood had in store for me.

I tell people all the time that's how my mom saved my life. I'm confident that, without that moment as a little boy, I would've killed myself at age 19, when the horribleness was at its worst for me. But the thought I held on to was, *If I can just get through this, I'll be able to see what God has been building me for.*

And as arrogant and hyperbolic as it may sound, I believe God was building me to team up with Adam and change the world through love. We've changed the solution focused field, and now we're carrying our message even further.

We believe you can change the world too.

When I'm told, "People can't change," I adamantly refute that statement. I remember how my life changed with one question and my mom's wise answer. *Wait a minute,* I realized. *I can be great.*

I started seeing people differently, people who were wonderful examples of change: Nelson Mandela, Malcolm X, Martin Luther King Jr., Barack Obama. I started paying more attention when I heard quotes like the one from Margaret Mead: "Never doubt that a small group of thoughtful, committed citizens can change the world; indeed, it's the only thing that ever has."

Take a moment to think of anyone that you deem to be a hero. Would that person be a hero if he or she hadn't gone through something difficult?

Cris Carter is a former football player in the NFL. Cris played great in college and was drafted by the Philadelphia Eagles in the 1980s, but he was eventually cut from the team because of alcohol and drug abuse. The Minnesota Vikings then picked him up through a waiver claim, famously paying only $100.

Cris cleaned up his life and worked harder in his career, eventually playing in eight consecutive Pro Bowls. He is regarded as one of the greatest wide receivers of all time.

In 2013, Cris was enshrined into the Pro Football Hall of Fame. During his speech at the ceremony, he said of his former Philadelphia Eagles coach, "Buddy Ryan drafted me. He tried to grow me up in the league. And actually what Buddy Ryan did was the best thing that ever happened for me, when he cut me and told me I couldn't play for his football team. But he told me a story. He told me the night before he went home and talked to his wife, and he asked his wife what he should do, and his wife told him, 'Don't cut Cris Carter. He's going to do something special with his life.'"

Although Cris was still cut, what his coach said motivated him to follow through and indeed become something special. He went on to play 12 years with the Minnesota Vikings, and by the time he left, he was their all-time leader in receptions (1,004), receiving yards (12,383), and touchdowns (110).

Through his example, Cris taught me that every good man has been through something. He helped me become proud of my trauma. It was *my* something. And I would use it to inspire others.

When people are at rock bottom, they have a tendency to think, *Why me? Haven't I been through enough hard things?*

But rock bottom can also be when you're at your apex. It's when people often dig deep and display their full brilliance. "Bring it on," they say. "I will not be dragged down anymore."

The strength to say "bring it on" comes from aligning yourself to your purpose. When you know your purpose, you rise. You can get through any difficulty.

In this book, we'll show you exactly how to do that.

BE ON THE LOOKOUT FOR CHANGE

A Closer Look with Adam

Sometimes people don't recognize the pivotal moments that spark change until later. In Elliott's example with his mother on the bus, he noticed change occurring quickly within himself. But other people may not be able to identify significant moments until they have more hindsight. Additional growth might need to happen for them to be able to look back and realize, "Oh, that was a catalyst for change. I just wasn't in a place where I could see it."

We encourage you to be on the lookout for change. Be purposeful about catching those pivotal moments and creating them.

For me, one of those moments occurred when I was in college. When I had been a premed student for two years, I had a nagging impression that I should change my major, and the major that kept coming to mind was psychology. Thinking it over, I literally laughed out loud. *I've never taken a psychology class,* I thought. *I don't know what psychology is. I'm not interested in psychology.*

A couple of weeks later, when it was time to register for the next semester, that nagging feeling kept pressing on my mind: *You should take a psychology class.*

I finally relented and signed up for a psychology class, not knowing that the thought I'd had was a pivotal change moment. I didn't realize it would change the trajectory of my life.

During that semester, I had to walk from my chemistry class straight to my psychology class, and there was a distinct difference with how I felt about each. I found that I hated chemistry, but psychology proved to be engaging and easy.

To make sure my interest in psychology wasn't a fluke, I signed up for another psychology class the next semester. At the end of that semester, I went to talk to my advisor. "I think I need to change my major," I said.

She looked through my records on her computer and replied, "You know, your timing is interesting because if you change your major right now, you can take less credits every semester and still graduate in the same time. Plus, with the classes you've already taken, you'll get a minor in zoology."

That sounded great. "Okay, I'll do it," I told her.

The psychology program wasn't as competitive as the premed program, and I was able to receive a scholarship. I no longer had to stress about money; I could focus on my education.

Even though it took me switching my major to realize it, all that was happening for me had been triggered by a thought I'd had months ago. But if I had been better at noticing the initial thought and feeling, I could have engaged with it differently. Instead of doubting myself for months, thinking things like, *No, I don't think psychology is for me,* I could have saved myself a lot of agony by engaging with my thoughts about change much sooner.

In psychotherapy, the word *insight* is often used to describe these kinds of pivotal thoughts. Sometimes it's an insightful thought, and sometimes it's a gut feeling. However that moment comes to you, it's a prompting for change, a moment when change feels possible, a moment intended to spur you to action, a moment that asks you to make a deliberate choice: either follow through or move toward the change in some manner, or don't and continue on your current path.

We'll be discussing agency, purpose, and your desired success at length in upcoming chapters, but for now, consider how they factor into deciding what changes you should make in life. For example, you have to decide, using your agency, whether to engage with a pivotal thought or feeling. Are you going to nourish it and help it thrive, or stamp it out?

Back in college, I could have thought, *I've already taken all these zoology classes. It's too late to change my major.* But I ultimately engaged with the insight I was having and acted on it.

Understanding your life's purpose can also serve as an anchor point if you ask yourself, *Does this insight or feeling align with my purpose or the success I desire? Should I foster it? Or should I let this prompting go by the wayside because it's inconsistent with my purpose and desired success?*

When I was a premed student in my first two years of college, if someone had asked me, "Why do you want to be a medical doctor?" I would have answered, "I want to help people." If I'd been more intentional about keeping that purpose in mind, I could have weighed it against my first prompting to consider psychology as a major. I could have asked myself, *If I follow through with switching my major, can I still be helpful to people?*

Yes, I could. Pursing psychology still fell in line with my purpose. If I'd been more intentional about understanding that, I could have saved myself months of doubt. Luckily, I was able to overcome the doubt and follow through with my promptings to make change.

GREATNESS REQUIRES DISCOMFORT

Diving Deep with Elliott

You cannot become your best self and stay comfortable. I don't think it's possible. What often holds people back from achieving what they desire is how it affects their comfort level. But you need to change your attitude so comfort isn't a variable. You have to be so focused on the outcome you're aiming for that your comfort doesn't matter.

Think of a woman who wants to be a mother. The process of producing a child can't be comfortable. The woman is going to experience nine months of discomfort, and then she has months of healing, during which she'll also lack sleep and have an infant who needs her care 24/7. But when she decides to be a mom, she has to accept that all that discomfort is just part of the process. She signs up for it.

Going to college is another example. I knew in college I wouldn't get much sleep, my brain would feel overloaded, and I'd always be on tight homework deadlines. But I went on that journey knowing I was choosing discomfort.

People aren't entitled to comfort, especially people who want to become their greatest selves.

Adam has been running every day for over two years now, and he still hates it. But if you asked him why he runs, he'll tell you about his visit with the doctor a couple of years ago when he learned he had high blood pressure. Now, his family has a history of heart attacks. His mom had one when she was only 37 years old. So, when Adam considers that his high blood pressure could cause himself to have a heart attack, it's very real. He thinks, *I could legitimately have a heart attack and leave my own family behind.*

He gets on the treadmill every day, not for himself but for his wife and three children. So, yes, getting on the treadmill hasn't ceased to be uncomfortable for him, but the meaning of that discomfort changes in light of the outcome he's after: to always be there for his wife and kids. The discomfort becomes something Adam is willing to take on instead of something to avoid.

Some of you might be thinking, *Yeah, but what I'm experiencing right now is uncomfortable. Depression or anxiety or feeling suicidal is a really uncomfortable place to be. I want to change my life to be more comfortable.*

But the reality is that you may not get to a place that is more comfortable. The discomfort becomes bearable because there's meaning to it if you know the deeper success you're ultimately after. As you work toward that, I promise you'll gain more than just discomfort. You'll experience joy, satisfaction, and purpose. Life won't just be "this is hard."

Overcoming your darkest moments leads to your greatest joy. You can't have one without the other over the course of your life, or else you don't appreciate what you have.

All that Adam and I have achieved together wouldn't have happened if we hadn't chosen the discomfort that came with elements of it. They created meaning and the opportunity to achieve joy. It wasn't just needless suffering, like when the racist attacks were happening to me, which I'll talk more about later.

Train your brain to not feel entitled to comfort. I credit my mom for teaching me that on the church bus years ago. Now I see the world differently.

A wonderful example of someone willing to endure discomfort for the greater good is Nelson Mandela. Think about how uncomfortable he was while imprisoned for 27 years. For the first 18 of those years, he was kept in a small cell without a bed or plumbing. He was forced to do hard work in a quarry. The only time he could write or receive a letter was once every six years, and once a year he was allowed one visitor for 30 minutes. Despite all this, his resolve to end apartheid in South Africa remained unbroken.

As difficult as all that was, think of how satisfying it must have been for him when he later became the first president of his newly democratic country. Mandela tore down South Africa and rebuilt it. Can you imagine how rewarding it must have felt was when he signed the country's rewritten constitution? I'm 100 percent sure if you talked to him and asked, "Was the discomfort worth it?" he would have answered, "Yes. For *this* moment." I'm also 100 percent sure if you had said, "Is the discomfort over?" he would have replied, "No. I've just trained myself not to attend to it."

VIEWING "PROBLEMS" AS PURPOSEFUL

Diving Deep with Elliott

I live in Texas, where you can become a licensed chemical dependence counselor (LCDC) without a master's degree. As long as you've received an associate's degree in chemical dependency counseling, have the internship hours, and complete the certification process, you can practice as an LCDC. During my senior year in college, I did just that, working at a halfway house. I was almost like a babysitter, just walking around with a walkie-talkie and making sure everyone was following the rules.

Half of this halfway house were residents in a drug treatment program, and the other half were men coming out of prison, reacclimating to the world.

At this halfway house, 12-step meetings were held pretty frequently, and they would invite guests to host them. One of those guests was a guy—I don't remember his name—but he was like a god among LCDCs. Everybody respected him. Multiple people said, "I got clean because he helped me."

One day I was talking to this guy about his story. He was hooked on heroin until his 40s. He didn't get clean until he went to prison. "When I got out, I was just finally done," he told me. "I had to figure out a way to stay sober, and service was one of the things that helped me. I decided to get a career in service, and now I'm an LCDC."

I remember thinking, *If anyone had stopped him from being a drug addict, they would have also stopped him from helping other drug addicts for the rest of his life.*

That was the first time I realized that maybe the job of counselors and therapists isn't to take someone else's problem away. We don't know why they struggle with what they do. Maybe our job, instead, is to help people become strong enough to deal with life as it's presented to them.

That perspective changes everything. If you can understand that you were given trials to face in order to do something beneficial with them, or because of them, later in life, then that gives your trials worth, meaning, and purpose.

On the church bus, my mom couldn't take my pain away. Instead, she helped me start to understand my pain had usefulness. I could learn from it, grow from it, and help others because of it.

THE GIFTS THAT COME WITH DIFFICULTIES

A Closer Look with Adam

Living with problems doesn't only give us a delayed benefit; there's an in-the-moment benefit as well, a reason to ask yourself, *What do I get out of feeling this way?*

I happen to live with a bunch of anxious people, including my youngest daughter, Julia, who is 12 years old. She'll say things like, "I have a stomachache, but I think I'm just worried about something." She is simultaneously our most thoughtful child, always aware of other people and what they must be feeling. She's also the most conscientious about saying thank you because she knows whatever another person has done for her was a sacrifice.

Julia's preoccupation with her own anxiety—what it feels like and how it's affecting her—extends outward, and because of it, she also understands what's going on with other people. On the other hand, my son who does not have anxiety is completely oblivious to what's happening to anyone else.

Because of the gifts, if you will, of Julia's anxiety, she's a better friend, a better sibling, a better child. When I'm out of town, she's often the only one of my children to reach out and say things like,

"How was the flight? Did you sleep well? Has the time difference affected you?"

My wife is also an anxious person, but we've realized that her anxiety matched with my laid-back approach to life makes us a more complementary pair.

For example, when we are planning a trip, she thinks about every contingency, and we arrive at our destination more prepared than if I had packed and made all the arrangements on my own. Because she's anxious, because she stews and thinks, because she stays up late and makes lists, the trip goes much better.

And then when we're on the trip, I can be my laid-back self and bring spontaneity and help us be more relaxed, no matter what we're doing. Again, we make a good team.

But people tend to think about anxiety as only a problem, when the reality is that it makes my child a more conscientious person, and it makes my wife a more prepared person. Those are positive qualities they wouldn't have if not for their anxiety.

A friend of mine took her 14-year-old daughter and her friends to their local roller-skating rink for her birthday party. This mom doesn't often see her daughter interact with friends because their house isn't the hangout house. Her daughter also struggles with anxiety, often complaining about how hard life is for her. But at the roller-skating rink, her mom watched in awe as she spent her birthday party asking her friends if they were hungry, if they needed anything, and even if they wanted to hold her hand while they practiced how to roller skate so they wouldn't fall. She was very attuned to her friends' needs, wants, and struggles, ready to help at every turn.

Sometimes people view challenges as something that's ruining their life. But consider this mom's daughter at the birthday party. One day she might want to have a partner. One day she might also want to have children. What skills is she developing right now to help her prepare for what's to come? She's attending to people who need to eat, she's offering a comforting touch to someone having a difficult time, she's standing beside someone who is learning something new.

My friend's daughter used to tell her that she didn't want to be a mom, but more recently she has said, "Well, maybe I could be a mom." When her mom asked what had changed her thoughts about it, the daughter answered, "I just thought for a long time that I wouldn't be any good at it, that I would be a bad mom because of how emotional I am and how anxious I get." But now she's starting to catch a vision of her capability. Her anxiety is shifting into something meaningful for her because learning to live with it is teaching her valuable skills. She's understanding that being anxious means she'll be a careful parent, an extra-loving and thoughtful parent as well as a parent who knows how to deal with exhaustion because anxious people are often exhausted.

Why would I want to take her anxiety away? If caring is a quality that comes from anxiety, I'd take anxiety all day long because that means I can care about people.

YOU DON'T NEED TO BE FIXED

Diving Deep with Elliott

I want to live in a world where people stop viewing problems as problems. If the girl in Adam's example were brought to my practice, I wouldn't want to fix her. Like Adam, I don't view her anxiety as a problem. It's just a circumstance she has to deal with. And I believe in my bones that God gave everybody a circumstance.

During a video podcast interview in 2018 with Kobe Bryant,[1] the interviewer discussed with him the ongoing debate of whether external factors, such as other team players and "the system," are responsible for the success or failure of new and hyped-up NBA players. Kobe Bryant replied, "That sounds like excuses to me. . . . Everybody has a different puzzle, man. You just gotta figure out your own puzzle."

That quote later inspired James Wiseman, a newer NBA player. After the Golden State Warriors chose him as the second overall pick in the 2020 NBA draft, Wiseman was only able to play a short while before he injured his knee and was sidelined for 18 months.

When interviewed for *Sports Illustrated*,[2] Wiseman said it wasn't the skeptics and critics who were causing him grief over his stunted career. It was "a battle within myself." He talked about struggling to get to the bathroom in the middle of the night on his crutches. "The only person that I [saw] in the mirror was me," he said. "So that means I'm in competition with myself. 'Okay, James, what you gonna do? You gonna respond? You gonna give up? Or are you gonna keep going through this and just stay strong?' And that's what I did. I stayed strong."

"Everybody got a different story," he went on to say, recalling Kobe Bryant's interview. "But [what] matters about the person is if you're willing to not give up and just go through it. I'm willing to go through it because I want to be the best."

For me, my puzzle is depression. I have to figure out how to deal with the depression and the trauma I've been through. But I certainly don't want it to go away because it's part of where my drive comes from. If you heal me from trauma, then you also heal me from passion and drive and compassion. And I don't want that.

As human beings, we have a tendency to believe we're entitled to a problem-free life. But even in the Bible it says we all have to deal with adversity. There's no perfect person with a trouble-free life. Maybe we should start viewing our flaws as just something we have to deal with rather than something we have to fix.

It's perfectly fine to own areas in your life where you can benefit from another person's greatness, all the while shining in what you do best. There's a reason opposites attract. That's why Adam is the ideal business partner for me.

I have no qualms about saying, "Hey, Adam. I'm going to go do these things because I'm a rock star at those, but can you do these other things that I'm not so good at and that cause me mental strife?"

With that kind of attitude, I don't have to fix myself because I'm not broken. I'm just not perfect.

PARADIGMS TO REMEMBER

- People can change.
- Change is within the realm of your control.
- Lasting change can happen in an instant.
- Evidence of change isn't always immediately apparent.
- If you want to become your greatest self, it's going to be hard and uncomfortable.
- When you know your purpose, you can find meaning in life's difficulties.
- There are no such things as problems. You only have circumstances.
- Dark moments create opportunities to learn valuable skills and achieve joy.

CHAPTER 2

THE HISTORY OF SOLUTION FOCUSED QUESTIONS

LOVE, EVOLUTION, AND MIRACLES

The solution focused approach, which is the basis for everything we'll share in this book, began in the most fitting way possible—with a love story. Its founders, Steve de Shazer and Insoo Kim Berg, came together as a couple 40 years ago, and 40 years later their relationship and legacy continue to inspire those in our field.

Both Steve and Insoo were psychotherapists. Steve was from Milwaukee, Wisconsin, and Insoo was from Korea but immigrated to Milwaukee. That's not where the two of them met, however.

Steve found his way to Palo Alto, California, and was training at the Mental Research Institute (MRI), where other therapists were doing pioneering work in systemic approaches to the helping professions, including working with families and focusing on communication.

The MRI became a remarkable place in our field. So many cutting-edge ideas were developed and experimented with there, spearheaded by leading figures in psychotherapy such as

Paul Watzlawick, John Weakland, Jay Haley, Donald D. Jackson, and more.

Insoo also went to the MRI to receive training, and that's where she met Steve. On the surface, the two of them had nothing in common—nothing that would have initially attracted them as a couple other than their shared interest in effective modalities of therapy. But as they continued to work together, their attraction built, especially a deep attraction for one another's minds.

Steve and Insoo's focus was on making therapy briefer. At the time, psychotherapy was synonymous with psychoanalysis, which involved a client coming to therapy two to three times a week for three to five years. Steve and Insoo, along with the MRI team, asked themselves one basic question: Can we make therapy briefer without sacrificing outcomes? The MRI team was able to reduce the average number of sessions down to about 10, a significant decrease from the traditional psychodynamic approach.

Steve and Insoo eventually moved back to Milwaukee, where they married and went on to create the "MRI of the Midwest," trying to replicate what was being done in Palo Alto. They opened the Brief Family Therapy Center, and from the research conducted there, they developed Solution Focused Brief Therapy (SFBT). Using this approach, Steve and Insoo were able to reduce the number of times a client came to therapy from even MRI's standard of 10 sessions, while still being just as effective at impacting a client's problem.

Steve and Insoo took psychotherapy and flipped it upside down and said that, instead of focusing on the problem or diagnosis or being reductionistic in how to view people, they were going to help them create lasting change in the most simple and direct way possible, all while being more efficient with their time.

From its roots with Steve and Insoo, the solution focused approach sprouted, and from there it branched out. One large branch developed in London in the 1990s and early 2000s at BRIEF, an independent training, therapy, and consultation agency for SFBT. The BRIEF team in London—Chris Iveson, Harvey Ratner, and Evan George—took the Milwaukee approach, but they wanted to see if they could make it even briefer.

In the same vein, we have taken the BRIEF approach and aimed to make it even briefer. In addition, we created the Solution Focused Universe, a worldwide training institute, and developed one of the largest current contributions in our field, the diamond approach to SFBT. We believe our diamond approach is the most efficient method of practicing SFBT.

Along with the mechanics of the diamond, what sets our approach apart is its stance—the position we take about viewing our clients as capable and strong and worthy collaborators in co-constructing effective therapy. In this book, we'll teach you to view yourself in that same light.

Like Steve and Insoo, we are very different but work together magically. And like them, we care deeply about people. We're trying to change the world by helping one person at a time.

The viewpoint that Steve and Insoo took about their relationship, their clients, and their life can be summed up best by the powerful yet simple mantra engraved on their shared headstone: believe in miracles.

We believe in the same. We believe in *you*. And one page at a time, we'll show you how to use the powerful solution focused approach in your own lives. By doing so, you'll cut right to the heart of what you desire most, and you'll view yourself as the mighty and skillful person you are that can achieve it.

HE'S THE DJ, I'M THE RAPPER

Friends before Colleagues

Diving Deep with Elliott

Back in 1988, actor Will Smith, who was then known in the rap world as the Fresh Prince, released a second album with DJ Jazzy Jeff, who would later become his co-star on the television series *The Fresh Prince of Bel-Air.* The album was named after one of its songs, "He's the DJ, I'm the Rapper." Whenever people ask me to explain the pragmatics of how Adam and I work together, that's what I think of: "He's the DJ, I'm the rapper," only, "He's the researcher, I'm the clinician." Each role is important and complementary to the other.

Adam and I came into the world of Solution Focused Brief Therapy at relatively the same time. When we met, I was excited to find someone close to my age and developmental phase who was bold enough to go against the status quo. He wasn't afraid to critique and expand upon some of the traditional methods in our field because he understood, like I did, that part of growth and analysis involves critiquing.

I think Adam was also happy to have met someone who was good at practicing SFBT because, as a researcher, he loved watching therapy but found it hard to find clinicians who were not only good at their work but also willing to record their sessions. I was happy to share mine.

That's why I always say, "He's the DJ, I'm the rapper." There are two definitive jobs in our partnership: researching SFBT and practicing it.

There was also a personal connection between us. I just liked Adam. Part of our interactions involved work, and we totally nerded out over it. But I was also keenly aware that I'd just met a very special person. We laughed and had fun together. We didn't just talk about work; we talked about faith, life, and family.

Another reason I compare us to DJ Jazzy Jeff and the Fresh Prince is because the DJ and the rapper were friends before they were artists. I'd say the same thing about us. Adam and I were friends before we were colleagues, and we will be friends through it all.

HOW WE MET

A Closer Look with Adam

Elliott and I met in 2008 at a conference in Austin, Texas, and were introduced by a mutual colleague. We just said hello, and that was it. Fast-forward two years, and the three of us—Elliott, our colleague, and I—all happened to be going to the same three-day conference in Malmö, Sweden, where we would be the only American attendees.

During the conference, we lost track of our mutual friend and started attending workshop classes together. At the end of the day, we went on a walk around Malmö to do a little sightseeing. We talked about things we liked or didn't like about what we'd been learning at the conference, and we realized we felt the same way about the solution focused approach—which happened to be very different from the way other therapists were practicing it.

"We should do a research study," I proposed. Elliott was hesitant at first—remember, he's the clinician, I'm the researcher—but I talked him into it. That got us excited, and we began to brainstorm other projects as well.

That walk together ended up being life-changing for us. Most importantly, it became very clear that our friendship should continue. Yes, we were on the same page about how we viewed SFBT, but beyond that we were laughing and having fun.

By the time we finished our walk, Elliott said, "I think we've just outlined 30 years' worth of work." Turns out it was much more than that. Eleven years later, neck deep in all we do together, we realize we have decades of work yet to come. Nothing is more exciting.

This book represents one of those exciting milestones. We're thrilled to share our groundbreaking approach to living a happier and more fulfilling life to more than just patients and other therapists. Now we get to share our message with *you*. Thank you for taking this journey with us!

TENACITY, BELIEF, AND LOVE

Diving Deep with Elliott

The foundation of SFBT is to believe in people, and I've always known that Adam believed in me. When he believes in someone, he's not capable of holding back his efforts to bring out the very best in that person.

After we got to know each other during that conference in Malmö, we scheduled weekly discussions with each other. This went on for two years, before we ever wrote or published anything. We did it because we enjoyed the conversation, we enjoyed the work, and above all we enjoyed the time spent together. Adam wanted me to realize my full potential, and I wanted him to realize his.

Solution Focused Brief Therapy became the vehicle for our friendship, and in many ways, that's what this book is about: friendship and love.

Adam and I decided long ago to use love as our tool, and we want the same for you. Understand that love—for yourself and others—is your power.

OUR SYNERGY

A Closer Look with Adam

Anyone who has met Elliott knows he's a very passionate person. Without him in the mix, my research might become overly intellectual, but he brings the passion and humanness to what I do.

Right from the beginning of our working relationship, there was a high level of excitement and trust between us, a mutual understanding of "I can tell you're doing your very best work, so I'm also going to do mine."

I'm sure we both would have been successful in our field without each other. We both would have been happy in our individual realms. But there's a synergy that comes when we're together. We're definitely better as a team.

Another defining aspect of our relationship is how we push one another outside of our comfort zones. Elliott is constantly dragging me into things I probably never would have done or have chosen to do, especially when they involve speaking in front of people. And I'm constantly dragging him into things he probably never would have done or would have chosen to do, such as diving into complex and ambitious research projects.

In the end, we're both grateful. If Elliott pulls me into something, I trust it's going to get infinitely better because we're doing it together. With him, anything can be enjoyable.

Regardless of who dragged whom into any given situation, by the time we're done, we always end up saying, "That was great! I'm so glad we did that!"

His strengths are different from mine, and mine are different from his. Both are important. Both are valuable. We completely respect that.

Elliott calls us the DJ and the rapper, but he also compares us to Batman and Robin. "Sometimes I'm Batman and you're Robin," he says. "And sometimes I'm Robin and you're Batman." We're both okay with either role. We're fine to let the other person shine.

ADAM'S STORY

My view of people and what they're capable of comes from my own experience of having to be strong during difficult circumstances, as well as witnessing the people close to me face significant challenges with great capability.

I'm the fourth of five children, and when I was very young, my mom went back to work full-time. She worked the night shift at the hospital, and she would put us kids to bed, go to work, and be back home before we woke up. We never felt the impact of her being gone, though it took a toll on her. For seven years, she worked throughout the night, getting very little sleep and pushing her body to the limit.

When I was seven years old, I woke up one morning and my mother wasn't home. My dad told me she was still at the hospital. She'd had a heart attack and needed open-heart surgery, he said. She was going to have to stay in the hospital for two weeks while she began her recovery.

That was a life-changing experience for our family, and I came to appreciate my mother in a new way as I watched her regain her health and energy. She learned to pace herself better, though she never surrendered her desire to continue accomplishing incredible things.

A few years later, when I was in middle school, my mother and father decided to go back to school to receive their doctorate degrees. They would not only be working full-time and going to school full-time, but my dad would also be serving as our church's stake president, a voluntary position in charge of overseeing several congregations across a large geographical area. Needless to say, my parents were very busy.

Many days would pass in which I wouldn't see them. My older sisters had grown into adults by this time and had moved out of the house, so my teenage brothers and I were the only ones at home.

I'm sure my parents couldn't tell you much about what happened during those years of my life. While I never viewed them as neglectful—they still provided for our needs and came to our school events—we were basically given free rein to govern ourselves. I had to learn very quickly how to become self-sufficient.

When I was 19 years old, I went on a church mission to England. I was given a calling to learn British Sign Language and work with deaf people. In doing so, I watched how the deaf community dealt with oppression and the pressure to assimilate from the hearing community, and how they rose to advocate for their own culture, equal opportunity, and fair representation.

Again, I witnessed the remarkable capability that people have in overcoming adversity. This became more evident than ever after I married my wife, Becca, in 2002.

Both of us wanted to start a family, but that turned out to be very difficult because she had horrible pregnancies with severe morning sickness. She was put on bed rest often and vomited five to six times a day on average. She suffered miscarriages too. Bringing children into this world was extremely taxing on her.

After she gave birth to our first child, I said, "If we never do this again, I totally understand." But she wanted more children, even though each pregnancy became progressively worse. I kept telling her the same thing, "If we never do this again, I totally understand."

The only reason we have three children now is because Becca fought so hard for them.

Later in our marriage, in May 2019, she was diagnosed with breast cancer. Our youngest child was eight at the time—the same age I had been when my mom had her heart attack. History seemed to be repeating itself.

Over the span of three months, Becca had surgery and four rounds of chemo. That was followed by six weeks of daily radiation treatments. She lost all her hair, dealt with excruciating pain (worse than her pregnancies), and struggled because she couldn't take care of her family—the thing she loves most about life.

In December 2019, she finished her treatments, but her cancer-related trials weren't yet over. In March 2020 (when the nationwide emergency was declared), COVID-19 hit our world. As a household, we had to completely lock down. Our kids didn't go to in-person school, even when schools reopened in our area. Becca's doctors explained that for a year following her cancer treatments, she would be immunocompromised. We had to implement strict measures to prevent her from catching COVID-19.

After nearly a year of isolation due to cancer and another year of isolation due to COVID-19, Becca has come out stronger and better. On the day she was diagnosed with cancer, I asked her how she knew she would be able to handle all this. She thought for a minute, cried for a few more, and then answered, "Because I can do hard things!" This became our mantra.

Recently, I asked Becca what life is like nearly two years after completing her treatments. She said she would never want to go through that again, but she is so grateful for the lessons she learned and the person she became as a result of these hard things. She mentioned that she appreciates the small things now, like being able to go to our kids' swim meets, going to the grocery store, and having the energy to stand up from a crouched position without feeling like she is going to fall over.

She also mentioned that even though her cancer and its repercussions were hard on our family, she is glad to know that we stand together and support each other. Now she has one more "hard thing" that she knows she can do.

As a husband, there is nothing worse than watching the person you love suffer so much, knowing there is nothing you can do to relieve the pain. Watching Becca push through challenge after challenge made me realize that she was proving not only to herself but also to me that she was stronger than we knew. Additionally, I realized that when we are the onlookers of other people during struggle, we are actually witnessing greatness. As people push through their hardest days, they manifest their greatest strength. Becca changed the way I see her, but more importantly, she has changed the way I see all people.

Elliott was also greatly touched by how Becca faced the challenge of cancer. He got a tattoo on his right wrist that says, "I can do hard things," written in Becca's handwriting. He is constantly trying to get me to get a tattoo as well, but so far, he'll just have to be satisfied with Becca's mantra in her handwriting.

Elliott has been there for me in both the good times and the hard. For over a decade now, I've had the privilege of being his best friend and business partner, and I've tried my best to support him as well.

The racism he's endured as a Black therapist in a white-dominated field has been staggering and horrifying. There were times he called me, having decided he was going to leave the field because of the mistreatment he received. However, each time we would talk about the bigger mission that he has and that we have together, and each time I committed to walk by his side again.

I am constantly amazed at his determination to teach people and to see the best in others, even when he isn't afforded that same courtesy. As with Becca's situation, I am often the onlooker while Elliott is the recipient of discrimination and oppression. But after 11 years, he just keeps getting more brilliant at his clinical work, teaching, and training, and he's living a generous life. It is an honor to watch his fortitude and ability "to do hard things"!

Where Elliott's adversity came firsthand, in many ways I was more of an observer of adversity. Perhaps my hardship in doing so wasn't as challenging as what my loved ones had to endure, but learning to remain hopeful during those difficulties has shaped who I've become, as well as increased my desire to research how meaningful conversation can access the greatness that is within the human soul.

While Elliott and I have confronted adversity from different angles, we've both reached the same outcome in our business and relationship—a united front committed to giving our very best to help people live happier and more purposeful lives.

FIGHTING RACISM AS BROTHERS

Appreciating Differences Has Been Our Greatest Strength

Diving Deep with Elliott

As a Black man in this field, I've experienced racism, exclusion, and discrimination—everything that goes along with being an overt minority. Adam, on the other hand, was in what we called "the club," meaning he was on elite boards and in contact with influential professionals, many of whom were actively oppressing me, though I didn't think at the time that he realized that.

Over time, he started losing access to the club. People began to exclude him from projects and started distancing themselves. Secretly, I felt bad because I knew the reason had to do with my working relationship with him, and I didn't know if he was aware of it. As bright as he is, Adam is very . . . well, white. Would he be able to piece together what was happening and why? Prejudice wasn't something he'd had to endure daily, while it was a reality I'd been living with my whole life.

Eventually Adam began to remove his own access to the club. He resigned from organizations and severed relationships. It took me years to conjure up the strength to finally say to him, "I think the reason that ugly things are happening to you is because of your association with me."

Without missing a beat, he replied, "I know."

"You do?" I asked, taken aback.

He explained that when he'd decided to work with me years ago, he knew what it would cost him. He even had a conversation with his wife about it—there are no secrets between them. "With my eyes wide open," Adam told me, "I decided to go down this path with you. And I don't regret it."

When I heard that, I broke down into tears. Essentially, he was saying, "I purposefully chose discomfort with you. And I'll continue to choose it with you."

Until then, I didn't realize the extent of how much he believed in me and how much he'd willingly given up in order for us to work together. It struck me that our relationship was more than a partnership of colleagues who happened to be friends. We were different. This was commitment. This was unequivocal loyalty.

Adam had all the acceptance in our field, all the privilege of it, but he ended up saying, "I don't want it. I would rather work with you."

A couple of years ago, Adam and I went on a trip to the American South and interviewed people who were involved in the civil rights movement. We met a guy named Hezekiah Watkins, who had been the youngest Freedom Rider at 13 years old during the Freedom Rides, a series of political protests against racial segregation on buses in 1961.

During our conversation, we asked Hezekiah what he thought of a Black man like me and a white man like Adam partnering together in the present day, given everything he had been through in 1961.

Hezekiah replied by telling us the story of how he'd been shot at when he was fighting for justice. "As I ran from the shooter," he said, "I looked to my left and saw a white guy running beside me. 'That's my brother,' I realized. His race didn't matter because we were both running from bullets while trying to create change."

I felt the same way when Adam said he knew what he was doing when he first embarked on this journey with me. He became more than an associate in that moment, more than a friend. He became my brother. He was willing to be shot at beside me—and he has been—fully aware of the consequences. Knowing he did it on purpose is the most touching thing I will ever experience.

Adam and I often say to each other, "I didn't know we could become any closer," and then something happens, and we inevitably do become closer. This was one of those moments. Our relationship became something more than it had been—and that something more has continued to grow ever since.

Adam is often mistaken for weak because he's small in stature and soft-spoken. But he's the strongest person I know. When people attempt to bully him, I sit back, pop some popcorn, and think, *Wow, this is going to be fun.* The man can't be intimidated.

He once resigned from a board that took issue with our project for racist reasons, and they had an exit meeting to try to pressure him to stay on their research committee. He was on that call for two hours, and if you know Adam, that call could have lasted for two years and he still wouldn't have backed down. When he believes he's in the right, he will not shrink. It's just not part of his character.

"I don't know how it happened," I say when people ask how he and I became what we are now. The only answer that seems to scratch the surface is, "God touched it."

While I don't know how it happened, I did recognize *when* it was happening—and that was the moment I found out he was willing to run from bullets with me.

For Adam to support me, I've had to authentically show him who I am. And for me to support him, he's had to authentically show me who he is. That has allowed us to simultaneously show the world who we are—and when doing that becomes hard, we're there for each other.

No matter what, I know Adam is at my side, saying, "All right, I've got you. Now go be you. When the bullets start flying, I'll be here, right here beside you."

PART II

The Stance: Reasons to Be Inspired by Yourself and Others

CHAPTER 3

ADOPT A NEW WAY OF THINKING

LEARN TO APPRECIATE THE BITTER AND THE SWEET

Diving Deep with Elliott

Most people don't walk through the world thinking about their own greatness and the impact they make and how wonderful they are. They're overthinking. They're worried. They're scared. But when you learn to put down your fear and pick up confidence, you tap into your true potential—the power you have to become your greatest self.

I'm obsessed with people like Jay-Z and Michael Jordan because of their level of confidence. For Michael Jordan, it's as simple as the knowledge that he's unbeatable. Jay-Z describes this kind of confidence as "the knowing."

During a lecture Jay-Z gave at Columbia University,[1] he said, "You have to have this knowing that, okay, it might not work today, it might not work tomorrow, but this is the right thing, and this is what I'm doing, and this is what's feeding me. That would be the best advice that I can give you, that 'knowing.' Just believe in what you're doing. And if you don't believe in it, then you're not doing it, and you haven't figured out what you do best yet."

The knowing is a higher level of faith. I want each of you reading this book to develop that higher level of faith in yourself and learn to find evidence of your skills and confidence. I want you to learn, like Jay-Z and Michael Jordan, to *know* it.

Think about a man who hates his job. If he hates his job, of course he's going to wake up every day dreading that he has to go to work. But what if this man could act on the paradigm that there are no such things as problems? He could focus on what he *does* enjoy about his job; he could learn to like things about it. He could also consider his life as a whole. He can think about his job in terms of the greater reward it provides for himself, for the partner and children he gets to come home to, for the comfortable place he has to live in, whatever the case may be.

I've learned to do this every day. I don't wake up thinking about the dozen people in my field who hate me. I've trained my brain to think, *Am I going to hear from the jerks today? Yeah. But I'm also going to talk to Adam and all the people who signed up for our trainings and those I'll get to meet when I travel.* That's a skill, I realize. Jay-Z does it. Michael Jordan does it. Kobe Bryant did it while he was alive. Their greater level of faith in themselves became their reality. Yours can too.

The outcome you desire will come by adopting a belief and then choosing the path of that belief—by walking in it, living it. In pursuing what you want, you become the kind of person who lives in the presence of it. You're inherently a better person, a more qualified person, a better partner.

Change is inevitable, but you can be in control of the kind of change you want to see in your life. Perhaps you won't take the pathway you thought you would to get there—the pathway being a new job in this instance—but you'll be happy with the person you're becoming. You'll ultimately realize that you've transformed; you've received your outcome.

The obstacle will always be present in your life. The man in our example will still have challenges at his place of work, but those challenges won't affect his confidence anymore. He'll feel appreciated, even if that's only at the hands of one or two colleagues or even just himself. He will have learned that happiness doesn't have contingencies. Happiness is the thing that goes in your pocket. You can take it wherever you go.

Adam and I were staying at his sister's house on a business trip we took to Utah. When I came out of my room the first morning, Adam's brother-in-law asked me, "Do you guys have a hard day or an easy day today?"

"All days are easy," I replied. That's genuinely what I think. Every day is a gift. My circumstances on any given day don't change that.

You might be thinking to yourself, *This all sounds great, but how do* I *get to a place where every day feels easy, and confidence comes with me?* Keep reading! Change comes with a changed mindset, which we're going to teach you all about in this part of the book, and then in Part 3 we'll teach you the mechanics of how to do it.

For now, know that there are only two kinds of days: good days and the bad days that give good days value. I get excited when I have what some people might consider to be bad days because they end up making me enjoy the good days even more.

I enjoy what Adam and I are currently achieving because I remember when it wasn't this way for us. If we had gotten our degrees when we were having the success we're having now, we would have no value for them. So, the fact that we had to fight to get here makes me wake up every day and feel awe and gratitude.

I tasted a fresh peach milkshake for the first time on that business trip I took to Utah with Adam. I didn't think I wanted one. I was tired, feeling full, and not craving anything sweet. But Adam's sister's family convinced me to try it.

When I took a sip, I thought, *Holy cow, this is the most delicious peach milkshake!* How did I realize the flavor was delicious? Because I've tasted other flavors of peach, such as the peach used in peach sparkling water, and that tasted very bitter to me. You have to experience the bitter to know the sweet.

Learn to love your obstacles because they help you savor the best parts of life. You can't have one without the other.

ENJOY THE JOURNEY

A Closer Look with Adam

As I mentioned in an earlier chapter, I served a mission for my church. When I returned home, I went out to lunch with two close friends to catch up. I asked them how things were going, and one of them said, "Life is just okay. It's just going the way that it goes."

And then my other friend said, "I'm preparing to go on a mission. I don't know if I'm actually going to go, but I know that if I prepare, I'll become the kind of person who would be ready to go, and I want to become that kind of a person."

That stuck with me. It's another example of what Elliott was just sharing, that you might not take the pathway you envisioned to arrive at your outcome, but in the disciplined pursuit of it, you'll receive your outcome all the same.

My friend might never have become a missionary, but she would have still become the kind of person a missionary is.

Let's say you want a million dollars. Well, you may not get a million dollars, but you might get the kind of life that a million dollars can afford, such as the security or peace, if those were reasons you wanted that kind of money to begin with. Perhaps there are also things that come with a million dollars that you *don't* want.

Ages ago, Elliott and I sat down and made a list of all the things we dreamed we could achieve by working together, and a couple of years ago, we realized we had inadvertently checked off everything on that list. It wasn't as if we were homed in on the list all the time, saying, "We've got to do this, and we've got to do that." We were just living life the way we wanted to live and saying, "We hope these things happen." By becoming the kind of people we wanted to be, the list took care of itself.

Now we find ourselves saying, "It's time to redream." The hard days in the past have helped us to appreciate these good days, and we can continue to appreciate the good and redream for more. It's a self-perpetuating upward cycle, and on the path toward the new dream, happiness and fulfillment are still present.

The truth is something we've all heard time and again: the joy is in the journey. The joy didn't magically arrive on the day we accomplished our outcome. Again, that realization came inadvertently for us. The joy was there all along.

As human beings, we're conditioned to think, that to desire change, we have to hate *here*, where we are in this moment. But that isn't true. You can find joy now, but also ascend to another place, which gives you permission to enjoy the journey.

Elliott and I enjoyed the journey when my wife had cancer, when he was being attacked racially, and when his house flooded. These were serious issues, but they didn't derail us in our purpose. They brought us closer together and made what we do, and all we hope to achieve, even more meaningful.

Elliott likes to talk about a very successful entrepreneur named Gary Vaynerchuk, more publicly known as Gary Vee, who wants to buy the New York Jets. The Jets are valued upward of $4 billion, while Vee's net worth is estimated to be around $200 million, so some analysts figure it could take Vee another 20 years to afford to buy the Jets.[2]

Despite this obstacle, Vee says, "The truth is, I just love the climb. I love the sweat, the long hours, the uncertainties, and the grind. Nothing in life comes easy . . . I've said it a few times before—the day that I actually buy the Jets is going to make me incredibly upset because the climb will be 'over.'"[3]

Train yourself to enjoy the journey.

ADOPT THE STANCE

A stance is a lens, a way of seeing people, including yourself. A stance isn't something to flip on and off like a light switch. It should remain on at all times. The stance we advocate in solution focused thought is one of being awe-inspired. We believe that you should live life in such a way that you are in awe of each person you meet.

Awe should be the filter through which each interaction should be processed. Awe might cause you to be astonished or surprised. Perhaps you see a small child who is outstanding at playing a musical instrument. This talent should surprise you, in the best of ways, but you should also be on the lookout for opportunities to be surprised—perhaps even asking children you encounter what special skills or talents they have, so they can surprise you.

At other times awe will take the form of amazement or wonder. This amazement might occur when you hear from someone that, despite having a physical disability, has risen to the top within a sporting event or they have tackled a physical adventure that many nondisabled individuals would never dream of attempting. You can be amazed by their ability to overcome hardship, but again, you should actively engage with people to be awestruck by them. You should hold a stance of awe, and you should engage with people from a place of awe within each interaction. The more you do so, the more you'll be able to be amazed at yourself.

Think about religion. It becomes a filter for those who practice it. Everything you do or think runs through it. The stance we ask you to take should also be a filter for your thoughts and actions. We want you to see greatness in yourself and others, and then act on that greatness. The stance influences your own behavior.

We created the acronym ADOPT to help you remember the stance and ingrain it in yourself. In order to master the diamond—the framework of solution focused strategies and techniques designed to help you achieve the success you desire—you must first ADOPT the stance. The five components of the stance are:

- A is for autonomy: autonomy is sacred.
- D is for difference: be difference-led.
- O is for outcome: be outcome-led.
- P is for presuppose: presuppose the best.
- T is for trust: trust your capability.

In the next few chapters, we'll discuss these five components in detail. Adopt the stance—truly accept it and let it change you—and you'll tap into your full potential.

CHAPTER 4

AUTONOMY IS SACRED

CAN I BLESS YOU WITH A HAIRCUT?

Diving Deep with Elliott

There's a cool celebrity barber named Victor Fontanez, who goes by VicBlends and has millions of followers on social media. Vic lives in Atlanta, where he walks around carrying a folding chair and his wireless barber equipment. He'll approach strangers on the street, including the homeless and former prisoners, and ask, "Can I bless you with a haircut?"

He sits them in his chair, cuts their hair, and has meaningful conversations with them. He asks them about their stories. He says things like, "If you could see something change in the world, what would you change?"

Victor wasn't always a famous barber. When he graduated high school, he attended barber school, which was scary for him at the time. He struggled to not compare himself to his best friends who were going to big colleges. But he stayed committed to his dream and got a "Barber Life" tattoo on his arm as a permanent reminder of what he wanted to do, even though that dream began with him cutting hair in his brother's garage with no air-conditioning.

"Whatever you gotta do to get your dream done, do it," he said when visiting his former high school as an alumnus. "The most important thing I did was start. As long as you start, you're doing more than most people."

When the COVID-19 pandemic hit, Vic was forced to stop being a professional barber, at least for the time being. "The one thing I was good at got [taken] from me," he shared when he was a guest on the Nick Cannon Show. "So now I'm sitting at the crib wondering who is Victor Fontanez if he can never cut hair again? Then I realized God blessed my voice long before he blessed my hands. You gotta reinvent yourself."

That's when Vic decided to take to social media to share his wisdom and videos of the free haircuts he was giving to strangers as they talked about life together.

I don't know how many hundreds of thousands of dollars Vic now makes every month because of how many followers he has, but fame and money couldn't have been his goal. His goal was cutting hair and sharing his message with the world.

"I'm a barber, but I feel like I'm not a barber at the same time," Vic told the students of his alma mater. "I feel like my voice is always going to lead me where I need to go."

Through following his purpose, by being obedient to it through humbleness and courage, many opportunities have opened for him.

Adam's story is similar. When he decided to switch his major to psychology, he made more than a great choice. He made a humble and courageous one. He needed to be humble to listen to his intuition, and needed to be courageous to act on it.

Humility and courage are what most people lack when they don't live in line with their purpose. Perhaps Adam could have been wealthier if he'd become a medical doctor, but riches weren't what he was seeking. Neither were hubris or status. He simply wanted to help people.

When I was growing up, I didn't want to be a psychotherapist. I thought psychotherapists were dumb. I wanted to play quarterback or third base. I had to develop humility to eventually pursue this field, and I also needed to become very brave.

Sometimes our instinct is to run away from the hard things we're meant to do. We're ultimately faced with the choice of fight or flight. I chose fight. Adam chose fight. VicBlends chose fight. And fight takes courage.

WHAT MAKES YOU TICK?

Diving Deep with Elliott

A while back, I conducted couples therapy for a husband and wife who had lived in Aspen, Colorado, and were now living in Keller, Texas. In Aspen, the husband thrived on hiking every morning, but Keller had no places to hike. Even if he had found a trail, the weather was too hot for hiking.

Without regular hiking in his life, the husband spiraled into a dark depression that almost ended his marriage. In order to preserve it—and the husband's life, for that matter—he and his wife chose to move back to a beautiful place where he could be outdoors daily. When they had moved to Keller in the first place, they didn't realize that they'd negotiated something out of their lives that was essential to the husband.

Everybody has that thing that, if taken away, would shatter them. In fact, most of the people who come to my office have negotiated something essential in their lives away. Don't fall prey to that temptation, even if your intentions are noble. Follow your own rules for happiness.

I worked with another client, this one a man from Australia, who was addicted to meth. Through one of our conversations together, he realized how important working on cars was for him. It was something he'd inadvertently stopped doing a few years previous and never should have negotiated it out of his life.

Why do cars make him tick? I have no idea. Do cars mean a thing to Adam? Nope. Adam couldn't care less about cars. If I said to Adam, "Wake up every day and work on cars," I probably just made his life worse. But for my Australian client, cars were what gave him oxygen. When he started working on cars again, he was able to get clean from meth.

For me, the thing I never want to negotiate out of my life is creation, whether it's writing, making videos, or creating any form of content. That's who I am at heart, a content creator, and I want to always be creating content to make people's lives better. That's my art. If you took creation away from me, I would suffer. Even before social media became prominent, I had a great need to express myself. I journaled all throughout my abuse as a child.

Figure out what makes you tick. It's part of who you are. It's what brings you joy and fulfillment. Never negotiate it out of your life.

HONORING THE ESSENCE OF WHO YOU ARE

A Closer Look with Adam

The traditional definition of autonomy is the right to govern oneself. Another word that goes with autonomy is *agency*, which means the right to choose. In solution focused thought, we fully believe in those rights. They're necessary for people to live up to their full potential.

When you honor your autonomy, you give yourself permission to be yourself—and you accept that who you are might not look like everybody else or what they want for you. As Elliott said, courage is required. You have to believe in yourself enough to know what you really want. What do you want to choose? How do you want to live? Once you value your own voice and your opinion, you need the strength to choose it, to live according to it.

Advocating for your own autonomy is going to come with discomfort. Learn to accept that as well as any negative consequences for following your own set of rules. But understand that honoring your autonomy will also come with rewards. You'll be free to be yourself. You'll experience peace.

Some people are debilitated by choice, by agency. They're concerned about how the choices they make will affect how others view them or how choices will affect their relationship with others. Pressure on how to live life, among other things, comes from worldviews, religious beliefs, political beliefs, and family beliefs. Consequently, people may assume that they need to adhere to a certain set of rules, which can make them feel trapped and unhappy.

In therapy sessions, a lot of our clients say they want to be a musician or an artist or whatever their dream occupation is, but their parents expect them to be doctors or lawyers or work the family business. Our clients feel conflicted between exercising their autonomy and pleasing the people close to them.

On the surface, autonomy sounds wonderful and blissful: *I get to do whatever I want! I can be my full self! I can live my full life!* But doing that requires courage, which involves discomfort. It also requires you to stand up to someone else to say, "I don't want what you want for me." That can put a relationship in a strained place, though hopefully just momentarily.

Valuing and honoring your autonomy comes down to honoring the essence of who you are. Other people might doubt you or encourage you to act otherwise, but if you acquiesce to their desires, you are giving up who you are. On the other hand, when you act consistently with who you want to be, you achieve peace. You choose to be the fullest version of yourself.

ACCEPT THE DISCOMFORT THAT COMES WITH AUTONOMY

Diving Deep with Elliott

When you don't honor your autonomy, you lose peace: Peace to sit in a room by yourself. Peace to be at ease. Peace to close your eyes and sleep comfortably at night. Peace that comes from being who you are despite external factors.

At times in my life, I've lived in the opposite kind of space, where peace doesn't exist because I'm acting in accordance to who everybody thinks I should be or who they want me to be. But to have peace, you have to figure out who you are and then become that person, whether people like it or not, whether they'll be upset with you or not, whether it will create discomfort or not.

When you share your dreams with other people, there will inevitably be those who root against you. But remember you're not entitled to comfort in life. Remember that greatness requires discomfort.

When you give yourself permission to dream, some people will be angry with you, especially when your dreams manifest and exceed their expectations. Why? Those people have placed limitations on you because they've placed limitations on themselves. If they predict that you'll fail and then you blow past that limitation, you've proven them wrong. And people don't like to be wrong.

Sadly, instead of being courageous and humble, some people are cowardly and arrogant. I've dealt with these kinds of people repeatedly in my life. When I've pursued a dream, they told me every step of the way I couldn't achieve it. But I did. I proved to them that just because *they* couldn't do it didn't mean *I* couldn't do it. I didn't let their doubts trample my faith.

Find the bravery to dream your dreams. Find the strength to live them. Support other people in their dreams. Resist the urge to hate those who surprise you with their capability. Do even better than that. Don't place limitations on others in the first place.

Above all, don't place limitations on yourself.

PEACE CAN COEXIST WITH DISCOMFORT

A Closer Look with Adam

We've been talking a lot about the peace and discomfort when exercising autonomy, so you may be asking yourself, *How can peace and discomfort coexist?*

Think about peace as a synonym for *assurance*. Going back to the example that Elliott shared in an earlier chapter of how I hate to run because it's uncomfortable for me, but I still choose to run because I feel an assurance that it's meaningful, that it will pay off in some way.

There's a difference between momentary comfort and the long-lasting assurance of why you're choosing to do something.

In the same way that momentary comfort and satisfaction are different from peace, fleeting happiness is different from joy. Joy is long-lasting. I have been in the throes of parenting struggles, like getting up in the middle of the night to change a leaking diaper or to clean up vomit, and was I happy in that moment? No. But when I looked at my child, when I felt the connection between us, I found joy. I found a lasting sense of "this is meaningful." You can endure times of unhappiness and experience joy.

Elliott talks about peace in terms of being able to look at yourself in the mirror and be proud of who you are. Choose to utilize your autonomy in a way that you can do so, no matter the discomfort that accompanies it. Utilize your autonomy in the vein of peace, assurance, and joy rather than the vein of temporary comfort, momentary satisfaction, and fleeting happiness.

CHOOSING WINNING OVER COMFORT

Diving Deep with Elliott

I've always been uncomfortable, which goes hand in hand with being African American. The more educated I became in life, the more uncomfortable I became because I found myself surrounded by an increasing number of affluent white kids. There aren't a lot of Black males in graduate programs, especially in my field. I've never had the expectation of comfort in my life. Instead of looking for comfort, I focused on winning.

I'm not talking about winning *against* people. Some people believe that to win, you have to defeat someone else. But a winning mentality doesn't mean that. It just means you're victorious over your obstacles. It means you accomplish your own goals. And I became good at breaking down my big goals into smaller goals, so it always felt like I was winning along the path to what I ultimately desired.

I was 11 years old when I decided I wanted to be a great baseball player and go to college. That way, I could have a scholarship and afford college, which was the only route I knew of getting there. I was also aware that great baseball players have pivotal moments that spur sports careers around ages 11 and 12. I knew it was time to get serious about the game.

I went to the big tryout in my community—I had just moved to Franklin, Massachusetts, and tryouts involved about 100 kids and 12 teams. After tryouts, the coaches held a draft to choose their players, and I got picked for the worst team. They were called Rotary Club, and they never won anything.

I was beyond disappointed. I'd played as best as I could, and I didn't make the all-star team. In Massachusetts, making the all-star team was a big deal because you got to play during both spring and summer seasons instead of only the spring, when lots of games were canceled due to the weather.

I remember walking to the field that summer, when baseball was over for me because the spring season had ended. The only kids who got to play now were the all-stars. As I watched these kids, I was furious. *Next year I'm making the all-star team,* I promised myself. *I don't care what it takes. I'm going to be an all-star.*

When the next year came around, I was leading the league in home runs. My batting average was amazing. I even led my crappy team to the town championship, and we won, a huge deal for a 12-year-old kid. I thought for sure I'd get to be an all-star.

But when the big tryouts came, the all-star team still didn't pick me. They only picked me as an alternate, which I knew was race-driven and political. For me to be one of the 12 kids chosen, a player from the previous year wouldn't get to be on the team, and all the kids' parents were very involved.

I didn't know I was an alternate until I went to my first all-star practice. One of the kids said, "What are you doing here?"

"Practice," I said, as if the answer was obvious.

"But you're an alternate." He frowned. "I didn't know alternates were coming."

Alternate? I thought. *But I'm the best player. My team won the town championship!*

Confused, I walked up to the coach and asked, "Am I an alternate?"

"Yes," he said, and it crushed me to the bone.

I left practice and went to a field near my house where kids liked to play soccer. I sat on a little hill there and watched them for hours, deeply hurt. When I finally went home, my mom said one of the assistant coaches stopped by and confirmed my position was indeed an alternate.

"I'm sorry this happened," he'd told her. "Elliott didn't deserve this. There was nothing I could do. But I'll make sure to get him involved as much as I can because he is awesome."

As difficult as that circumstance was, it was also when I formed a winning mentality. I resolved that, for the rest of my life, I would work as hard as I could so that only two outcomes could result: I'd achieve the goals I set out to do, or I'd work so hard and perform so well that everyone would know I was cheated if I didn't achieve what I was after.

To this day, that is what drives me. It doesn't matter what it takes. I'm going to do my ultimate best so that it's plain to the world that I have justly earned my dreams, even if they're temporarily cheated from my grasp.

As a 12-year-old kid, I took discrimination and used it for fuel. "I'm going to give them both barrels," I started to say, meaning I'd give everything I possibly could to make my worth obvious.

The all-stars finally drafted me the next year, when I turned 13. But even if they hadn't, I would have maintained my winning mentality. My strong will was forged when I was 12 in that moment of blatant and unfair rejection. The pain was so horrible that I decided I would never let it overcome me again.

Let me reiterate that winning is not about an adversary. When Adam and I entered the field of psychotherapy, I didn't realize I was 10 miles behind him because I am Black. I want to stand next to him. I don't want to trip him. I don't want to sabotage him. I don't want him to lose. But if Adam has access to that stage, dammit, I want access to that stage too. That means I need to win against every obstacle in my way. It doesn't matter to me if I have more obstacles than Adam. That's irrelevant. I've still got to get past them. I've got to do whatever I can to own the space side by side with him. To me, that's the winning.

Learn to win in your own life. Believe in your self-worth. Demonstrate who you are at every turn, despite any obstacle that crosses your path. Win for yourself, not to make others lose but to achieve your goals. Keep your bigger dream in mind while you work hard at all the steps it takes to get there. Each milestone you reach is praiseworthy and necessary, no matter how small it may seem. When you recognize your success at every level, you'll see how your journey is a winning one. Your self-worth will grow, and the upward cycle will repeat. Don't let any doubts or disbelievers break your momentum. You have what it takes to succeed.

DRAWING ON STRENGTH INSTEAD OF DRIVE

Diving Deep with Elliott

Greatness requires being stubborn in your persistence to walk your path. I've never met a strong person who didn't have a difficult life . . . until I met Adam. Confused and fascinated, I used to ask him, "How are you so strong but have had a relatively smooth life?" Not a perfect life, obviously, but it didn't seem very rocky.

For me and all the heroes I'd ever had, strength always come from fire. We pulled ourselves out of poverty and other extreme difficulties. But Adam was different. He had strength without fire. He didn't have the story of "I had to walk to school uphill both ways."

Despite that, he still had the ability to say, "I don't care what the world thinks. I'm going to do what I want because I think it's right."

Thanks to Adam, I've had to reconfigure how I believe strength develops. I still think it comes from struggle, but I no longer believe struggle is the only path there. In Adam's case, I learned that his fire is his faith. He's not driven the way other people are, including myself.

Now, obviously Adam is very accomplished, and you can't be accomplished without being driven. But driven, as I've seen it in many businesspeople, usually entails excessive behaviors, such as people who don't sleep and have had multiple divorces. Their drive trumps everything else in their lives. But what makes Adam a superhero is his incredibly high level of strength and self-awareness.

People underestimate him because he is small, soft-spoken, and shy, and they'll test him at times. When that happens, I jokingly say to Adam, "I'll just get my popcorn and watch." I know how the interaction will end—those people will learn how immovable Adam is. They won't see it coming either because strength doesn't always look like the package Adam presents.

There's a spiritual root to Adam that holds him firm to what he believes in. If he had to make a choice between giving up his principles and losing his job, he'd choose losing his job. He would rather go be a cashier at a grocery store and stay true to himself. An ambitious person wouldn't do that.

Adam goes to bed at 10:00 every night because he knows he wants to wake up at 5:00 or 5:30 in the morning for a specific reason. There's a purpose to each choice he makes. He has a very self-aware vision for his life, and he's willing to sacrifice now for the payoff he wants later. What Adam won't sacrifice, though, is his relationship with his wife and children. Driven people often succumb to that, but Adam's strength holds him in check.

His purpose, as he defines it, is to become the best version of himself, and that version is someone who prioritizes his family and God. Adam exercises his autonomy to align with that purpose, and he won't act on something if it isn't good for his family and what he believes God wants for him.

Ask yourself what fuels you to follow your purpose. Are you driven like me or strong like Adam? Neither answer is wrong, but if you're driven and ambitious, learn to keep that in check with your purpose—what you value most in life. Likewise, if you draw on strength, continue to feed it with what makes you strong, whether that's family and faith, like Adam, or other kinds of relationships and reasons. Find your fuel and keep it burning.

REFUSING TO TAKE THE TEST

A Closer Look with Adam

I took a lot of honors and advanced placement (AP) classes in high school, one of which was an AP English test during my senior year. English wasn't my strong suit, so I knew if I wanted to get better at it, I'd have to take it again in college. Consequently, I decided that taking the AP test was a waste of time and money. I wasn't going to do it.

"I noticed that you didn't sign up to take the test," my English teacher said, pulling me aside one day.

"Yep," I replied.

"But I think you could pass."

"Maybe," I conceded, sensing her growing irritation with me. "But I want to learn this content again."

Looking back, I realize she would have gotten better reviews and more money if a larger number of her students passed the test. She definitely had an incentive, although I didn't realize it then. But I stayed firm in my resolve to not take the test.

A couple of weeks passed before she brought the matter up again. "If money is the issue," she said, "then the school will cover the cost of your test."

"I don't need to take the test," I replied. "I don't *want* to take the test."

She persisted, saying I *did* need to take the test, but I knew I didn't, so I held my ground. I reiterated that I wasn't going to do it.

The day of the test arrived, and all students were required to go to our English classroom, whether or not they were taking the test. I showed up as 1 of the 3 out of 35 students who weren't taking it. We had to wait in the classroom while everyone else left to wherever the test was being administered.

The test was supposed to start during the middle of our class period. Just before then, my teacher approached me once more. "We ordered an extra test, Adam. So, if you'll just go take it, you can be done. You'll receive your English credit in college."

"I don't want to take it," I said, sounding like a broken record.

And at this point, she was beyond irritated with me. Again, I didn't understand what was going on for her. "If you don't take the test," she said, fuming, "I will give you a B."

I couldn't believe she was threatening me by lowering my grade just because I wouldn't take an optional test. I knew I had earned an A in that class.

"Just go take the test!" she shouted.

"I don't want to take the test!" I repeated for what I sincerely hoped was the last time.

I never did take the test, and so my teacher followed through with her threat and gave me a B. I was a straight-A student all through my senior year of high school except for that one B in English on my report card. I don't regret how I earned it.

Although my teacher tried to make saying yes as easy as possible, I used my agency to say no. For the most part, my teacher's intentions were good, and her confidence in me was appreciated, but I wanted to learn more about English in college. I didn't want to skip that opportunity.

When I did go to college, I took a technical writing class that became one of my favorite classes, something I never would have guessed based on my high school experience with English.

In the end, I'm glad I stuck with what my agency was telling me to do. Acting on intuition like that represents who I am and how I've continued to live my life.

My story isn't as dramatic as Elliott's story about baseball and how that was a defining turning point in his life, but for me, small and pivotal moments like refusing to take an easier route because I wanted something even more worthwhile illustrate how I operate.

I'm careful about the decisions I make, and once I make them, I'm going to stick with them.

Can you think of a time in your life when you went against the status quo to choose something better for yourself, when you followed your own set of rules to pursue what you felt was best? How did that change you and strengthen you? How can you draw from that same courage again to make more brave choices in your life, choices that lead you toward what you desire most?

HONORING YOUR AUTONOMY VS. BEING SELFISH

A Closer Look with Adam

When people don't honor their own autonomy, they often do so for what they believe is the best of reasons: to accommodate someone else, to be polite, to sacrifice for others, or something similar.

Think of stay-at-home moms. Some feel complete in that role, but others feel like they've given up their careers to be home with their children. They begin to feel like being a parent isn't rewarding, and it turns into drudgery.

But it's possible to achieve a balance between what fulfills others—in this case, caring for a child as a parent—and what fulfills a person, what makes them tick and provides the joy that is lacking. Sometimes people err too far on one side or the other of what other people need versus what's fulfilling for them when they exercise their agency.

For me, the thing that makes me tick—the thing I wouldn't want to negotiate away—is a balance between my family and my alone time. I do a lot of things with and for my family, but I'm also an introvert, so I need my personal space as well.

I like to wake up early in the morning to start my day, partly because my house is absolutely quiet at that time. Many of my family members like to stay up late and are still sleeping before dawn, so I can do whatever I want then. It's how I recharge, even in short doses.

A while ago, my family went to visit our friends at a lake house. I had too many things going on so I couldn't go with them. Staying home alone turned out to be rejuvenating for me. I felt a lot of peace and calm and quiet. I'm a person who likes structure, order, and organization. I need my space to be chaos-free. But I also need to balance that between time spent with my family, which also fulfills me.

When I was in grad school, I was gone from home a lot, always busy with work and deadlines. My kids were little back then. Toby was born in the middle of my doctoral program, so by the time I finished, he was about 18 months old, while Rachel was four and a half. I used to tell people, "My kids are my best barometer if the balance is off in my life." That was always easy to figure out because my kids would say, "You're always gone, Dad" or "We haven't seen you lately." When that happened, I knew I needed to slow down the work and give them more attention.

My family means everything to me. They're the driving force in what I do, but I also need individuality. But if I just choose individuality in my life, I am only honoring my own autonomy. I refuse to do that because I don't live in a vacuum. No one does. There are people within my realm that I'm responsible to and for. If I only look out for myself, I violate the autonomy of someone else. That's what selfishness is—valuing what you want more than what another person wants or needs.

Valuing autonomy isn't person-specific. It isn't case-specific. If you truly honor autonomy, you must value your autonomy as well as the autonomy of those you're close to. When you choose to be in a relationship with another person, whether that's romantic, familial, or business-related, you're also choosing to value the autonomy of that entity you've created.

Negotiating a balance is so important. Ask yourself how much you want what you want in life. How much do those close to you want the same? Partners need to decide things together, like where they are going to live, whose family they will visit on holidays, what traditions they want to keep, and what traditions they want to create.

Selfishness comes from valuing only your own autonomy. Unhappiness comes from only valuing the happiness of others. Don't fall in either trap. Finding the balance is what keeps relationships healthy.

THE TROUBLE WITH PEOPLE PLEASING

Diving Deep with Elliott

In addition to being unhappy, if you only value another person's autonomy, you become a people pleaser, and that gets you into trouble. I see people pleasers all the time in therapy. They'll come in after 10 years, 15 years, 20 years of people pleasing and suddenly realize, "I have this entire life that I don't want because all I do is please others."

An example of this is that I want to move to Toronto, so naturally I brought it up to Adam, trying to get him on board. "How cool would it be to live in the same city together?"

"Yeah, I don't think so," he replied. "Becca doesn't want to live in a cold city again." That's him valuing her autonomy. He's essentially saying, "I don't have one thought or another about Toronto, but my wife does, so I don't think I can do it."

Now, if it were just up to Adam, he'd say, "Sure! Toronto sounds great. I don't want to live there forever, but we could live there for a few years. Why not?" But if he acted on that, that would be very selfish. He'd be making the choice based on his autonomy alone. He won't do that because he's connected himself to another person, Becca, so he's going to honor her autonomy.

There are other times, however, when Adam has to advocate for his own desires. If Toronto were the dream place he's always wanted to live, this scenario would play out differently. He'd need to have a serious conversation with Becca about moving there.

In your valued relationships, learn to negotiate a middle ground that values everyone's autonomy. Don't live a life only pleasing other people or only pleasing yourself.

LEARNING TO DELAY GRATIFICATION

A Closer Look with Adam

This chapter is titled "Autonomy Is Sacred," and sacredness means something that is valuable, something that's worth saving for special moments, something worth sacrificing for. To fully understand how to honor autonomy, you need to connect it to what you desire the most. If that something is important enough, it's worth delaying your gratification for.

Think of delaying gratification in terms of "I can give a little here—I can sacrifice my autonomy for this small circumstance because I know in the long run it's going to lead me to something else that I want more." You temper what you want in this moment for what you want long term.

Several years ago, Becca and I were living in Oregon, which was beautiful and wonderful, and then we had to consider moving to Lubbock, Texas, where I could pursue a very good Ph.D. program.

"This place is horrible," I told Becca on a phone call during my visit there. "It's ugly. It's the worst place I've ever been. But I think it's the right place for us to be right now." I gave her the reasons and helped her envision what it would be like if we lived there.

Unlike the scenario Elliott gave of me moving to Toronto with him, which I felt indifferent about, moving to Lubbock for a while was actually important to me and my career. I had to advocate for my autonomy and say to Becca, "For the long-term plan, this is the best option for our family." Thankfully, she honored my autonomy with her response: "Okay, let's do it."

Becca did not want to move to Texas, and she did not like living there (although she made some important, lifelong friends). But she honored my autonomy as well as our relationship's autonomy, knowing we had a shared desire of the ultimate place we wanted to arrive at together, and my Ph.D. program in Lubbock put us on that pathway there.

Now we live in a beautiful part of Georgia, where we moved to years ago when I started working for a university. We've been here a long time, but a large portion of Becca's family lives in Utah. One of the things Becca has started to realize in this part of her life is that being around her family is essential to her happiness, especially after her isolation due to COVID-19 when she was recovering from her cancer treatments. We're currently trying to work out a balance to honor what Becca wants now.

We want to get our kids through school in Georgia before we move again, but in the meantime we've determined to get Becca to Utah more often because she needs being near family to fill her up. That's what makes her tick.

In essence, the balance has shifted from the needs of my career to focusing on what Becca is advocating for. Now we're reprioritizing. These variables are always going to shift in relationships, or in our case, our family. We have to consider not only what each of us desires but also the needs of our children.

As you can see through the various examples in this chapter, honoring autonomy takes work. You might have to endure discomfort to value someone else's autonomy. You might have to work hard at figuring out the balance between what you want and what a loved one does. Circumstances will always change, so you need to be constantly aware and constantly negotiating how to find the right balance of autonomy.

Questions to Ask Yourself about Autonomy

- What values do I have that I don't want to compromise with anyone about?
- Do I believe that my opinion/wants are as important as anyone else's?

- What am I willing to do to defend my desires and needs?
- Am I willing to let others (partner, children, friends, parents, etc.) make their own choices and decisions without feeling angry or frustrated with their decisions?
- What can I do to improve on honoring my own autonomy/agency?
- What can I do to improve on honoring the autonomy/agency of others around me?

CHAPTER 5

BE DIFFERENCE-LED

THE PITFALL OF NOT CHANGING YOUR WAY OF THINKING

Diving Deep with Elliott

Did you know that approximately 70 percent of people who suddenly receive a huge windfall of cash lose it within a few years?[1] They burn through it quickly, spending it frivolously. They divorce. They become addicted to drugs. They commit suicide. They end up unhappy or broke. Their lives are worse off instead of improved. Why? They didn't learn to think differently.

If you give a broke person 10 million dollars and he doesn't learn to stop thinking like a broke person, he will eventually become a broke person again. Even worse, he'll become a broke person with regret and remorse because now he lives with the memory of knowing he squandered 10 million dollars.

Whatever you want in life, you better be damn sure to change your way of thinking, or the basis of your life won't change, even if you temporarily obtain the surface-level thing you've desired. In the rap song, "Uptown Anthem," by Naughty by Nature, one of the lyrics is "No matter where you go, there you are."

People fall into the trap of thinking, *I'll be happy when I get what I want.* They place contingencies. Let's say what you want is a new job because of something negative you're dealing with at your current job. Then you get a new job, and you expect life to be fixed and enjoyable. When it isn't, you spiral into hating life all over again. Why? You didn't change your thinking. You didn't hold on to the meaning of what you want and you didn't learn to view obstacles differently.

I was so excited to start practicing psychotherapy, and my first job after receiving my bachelor's degree was working as a case manager at an agency in Fort Worth, Texas, where clients had to be below the poverty line. I did very well there. My clients loved me and referred me to others, so my work was in high demand.

A woman named Jackie worked at this same agency. She was a privileged woman from the South, and she had a case manager job like I did. Jackie hated me for the love and accolades I got from my clients, so she made my job very difficult. She was the first politically driven person I'd met in this field, and she feared I was after her job she ultimately wanted—to be promoted to administration and run the clinic.

To set things straight, I pulled her aside one day and said, "Look, Jackie. I just want to make it clear to you that I only want to be a clinician here. I know the management likes me, but I promise that if they offer me a promotion that takes me away from seeing clients, I won't take it." I tried to assure her I wasn't after the same opportunities she was, but she still persisted in hating me and doing everything she could to make me miserable there.

I eventually thought, *I've got to find another place to work where there's no Jackie.* I resigned and found a different job at an adolescent services clinic, where the executive director was essentially another Jackie. I didn't understand how someone in so high a position could find me threatening, but she did, hating me just as vehemently as Jackie did. I quit and went to work for another agency, where it just so happened that Jackie's husband was also employed. As you can guess, he wasn't an Elliott fan.

This whole time I kept thinking, *If I could just find a job without a Jackie.*

I decided to open a private practice because surely there could be no Jackie in an office I owned. Soon I met Adam and we started traveling around the world and training people about Solution Focused Brief Therapy. And guess what? I met a dozen more Jackies.

That's when I realized the answer wasn't about finding a place without a Jackie. There isn't a corner of this world without a version of her in it. If I went to Antarctica, there would be some penguin hating on me. What I needed to do is make the Jackies in my life not matter.

I trained my brain not to focus on the haters and to instead focus on what I enjoy—getting to spend time with Adam and those who appreciate me while sharing messages I believe in that make a difference in other people's lives.

You need to do the same thing. You're never going to get through this life obstacle-free. It isn't meant to be a smooth ride. Train your brain to accept the obstacles. Don't focus on them; that will only give them power over you. Instead, focus on becoming indestructible. Focus on what you do enjoy. Focus on being grateful. Focus on where you can make an impact in this world, no matter how big or small. Focus on what you do have control over, even if that's only your own thoughts and actions.

THE DIFFERENCE OF BEING YOUR BEST SELF IN ALL YOUR ROLES

A Closer Look with Adam

There are different versions of us. Take me, for example. Among other versions of me, there's a dad version, a husband version, an employee version, and a churchgoing version. I'm still the same person; I just have different requirements—different skills and postures—that I utilize in those different roles. For example, I show up very differently for my children from how I show up for my wife.

Adopting a difference-focused lens is important to solution focused thought. We're interested in the differences within the roles each of you have and how they link to the person you desire to be. Ask yourself, if the very best version of yourself showed up, who would that be? What qualities would you have? What characteristics? How would you want people to respond to you and interact with you?

Once you have a clear vision of that best version of yourself, imagine how you'd interact with your kids, knowing that you have a certain role as a parent to them, but now the best version of you is present. What would you do differently? What would they notice about you? Now ask yourself the same questions about differences you'd notice in other roles of your life, when you also show as your best self.

Let's say you want to be less depressed. Instead of focusing on what depresses you, think of how you would react differently to a distressing or depressing circumstance when you show up as your best self. Likewise, if you want to be more confident, ask yourself what you know about this best version of yourself that would show differently when you need to be confident.

When you envision the best version of yourself, you may think things like, *I want to be less anxious, less depressed, and less shy.* But those thoughts are focused on what's absent from yourself, rather than what you want yourself to be.

Instead of dwelling on what you lack, ask yourself difference-oriented questions. What would you rather be if you were less depressed? What would be there in its place? What would you be instead of less depressed if you were less shy? What would be there instead?

In essence, you should ask yourself, "Instead of whatever is happening to me, what would I like to be there in its place?" That question is one of the best ways to describe who you desire to be and what you want to obtain. The more vividly you can define and visualize those things, the more likely they will manifest in your life.

THE DIFFERENCE IS THE MEANING

Diving Deep with Elliott

We all know the thing we want in life, the thing that's most important to us, and that is what I view as difference. It's the difference we're pursuing, the difference that matters. But difference goes so much deeper than that. You can continue to define and articulate what matters the most to you—what you want the most—by asking yourself endless questions about how having that thing in your life would make a difference to you. Difference is what reveals its meaning. In other words, the difference is the meaning that surrounds what you want.

A desired outcome (what you want the most) could be an ice-cold drink. But what difference would having an ice-cold drink make to you? Why is it meaningful? That's a simple example, but it illustrates my point that people often only think about their thirst (what they're lacking or what they want on a surface level) rather than the joy and fulfillment of obtaining their desired outcome.

Questions about difference are important because they break down that meaning to the smallest details. When you can deeply envision those details and how they will play out in your life, you become the person who can make them a reality.

Over the years, I've seen a lot of young adults in therapy sessions. They often begin by saying something like, "I don't want to do school anymore."

"What do you want to do instead?" I'll ask. In other words, what do you want to do differently?

"I want to sit at home and play video games," they might reply.

Well, they just chose to be fat and lonely for the rest of their lives because they don't understand the meaning of their decisions.

"What do you want to achieve in life?" I'll ask, trying to help them dig deeper.

"I want to be a dentist," they'll say, or some similarly lofty outcome.

Those answers are always interesting because not going to school and playing video games is counterproductive to that desire of what they want to become. I'll continue to ask more difference-led questions to get at what they really want by becoming a dentist and from there help them envision the steps to pave the way.

Adam and I will explain how to do this more in the diamond chapters of the book, but for now let's keep focusing on difference.

I'm good friends with the comedian Tiffany Haddish, who has a clear understanding of the concept of difference. In my opinion, Tiffany sits on the Mount Rushmore of comedians. She's one of the most accomplished out there. And she has known what she's wanted since she was 10 years old.

Tiffany had a horrible childhood that involved abuse, foster care, and abandonment. That's her trauma. But when she was 10, somebody told her if she could make people laugh, people would like her. In that moment, she decided she wanted to become a comedian.

In relation to what we're talking about, Tiffany's desired outcome was to be a comedian, but the meaning around it—the difference it would make in her life—is that people would like her, which soon evolved into a deeper difference: "My job on this planet is to administer joy," she recently told me.

Tiffany isn't perfect by any means—she's the first to admit she's a flawed person—but I've told her she has a superpower, which is that meaning is constantly a part of her. She draws strength from thinking along the lines of "I'm not just doing this for me in this moment. Here's the bigger picture and the larger impact I want to make."

Tiffany and I were at a festival once, where she set up a table for her foundation, the She Ready Foundation, whose mission is to inspire, protect, and provide resources to youth impacted by foster care. On the table, prizes like bracelets, candy, and little trinkets were displayed. Kids who stopped by and answered enough trivia questions could choose a prize.

One of those kids was a seven-year-old boy. After surveying all the prizes, he eyed a big suitcase on the table. "I can have *anything* on the table?" he asked Tiffany's assistant.

"Anything," she assured him. He chose the luggage.

Later I asked Tiffany, "Why was luggage on the table?"

She told me that when she was first put into foster care, the social workers made her shove all her clothes into trash bags to make the move.

"I literally thought I was garbage," she said, "just being moved around from people to people, from house to house." Each time she was required to use trash bags. "And then one day somebody gave me a suitcase, and it changed my whole perspective on who I was."

How you view yourself matters. After Tiffany got that suitcase, she began to view herself differently. She started to think of herself as a traveler. She believed she was on an adventure, that she was a visitor in these people's homes, as opposed to being garbage dropped off at their doorstep. Before then, every time she was moved to a different place, a lot of her stuff was thrown away. She felt like she was always losing. "But when I got that suitcase," she said, "and *my stuff* was in *my suitcase* for *me*, then I felt like I was on an adventure. I'm a visitor. I'm a traveler. I felt like my whole life changed."

Tiffany decided when she was 13 that if she ever got some power, she would make sure no one felt like garbage. *Children shouldn't feel like trash,* she thought.

She found work at a youth center, where she discovered ways to fundraise so the foster kids could have their own suitcases. These were little fundraisers at first, but when Tiffany was cast in her first TV show and obtained fame, she expanded her fundraising. She decided that if anyone wanted to take a picture with her, they would have to donate a suitcase.

That evolved into Tiffany getting truckloads of suitcases for foster kids. Now she says if people make a donation to her foundation or if they buy any merchandise, all proceeds will go to getting more suitcases for these kids.

"The transformation I've seen in young people from something as simple as a suitcase," she told me. "Because it gives them a sense of purpose."

In one moment, Tiffany went from viewing herself as trash to a traveler—and look at where she's traveled. Her great gift for comedy led her to fame, and with that fame she continues to provide ways for other foster kids to become travelers too.

Comedy is not Tiffany's greatest gift. Inspiration is.

With one suitcase, she found meaning in her life. She found what made the difference. And now she helps children everywhere find that difference for themselves too.

Difference isn't about the immediate reward. Tiffany could have wanted to become a comedian for very different reasons, and those reasons could have never evolved into helping others, which is what brings Tiffany joy. But she had vision. That's what difference is about—the vision beyond merely getting what you want. It's what getting what you want *means*.

Obtaining your desired outcome impacts more than just yourself. It impacts relationships and society. It's a ripple in a pond that continues to expand outward in its benefits.

What will be the impact of your desired outcome in the lives of others? What will be the difference you make?

THE THREE LEVELS OF DIFFERENCE

A Closer Look with Adam

Solution focused thought is about difference and its many layers of meaning in your life. In the first level of difference, you ask yourself, "If the best version of myself showed up, what would I notice? What would be different? What signs would manifest to let me know that this version of myself is here?" In other words, "What differences would I see?"

In the second level of difference, you ask, "What difference would it make?" If you started to see confidence show up, or if you started to see anxiety decrease, what difference would that make? What you're really getting at by asking, "What difference would it make?" is how would it impact you? How would that change the way you show up?

In the last level of difference, you ask the meaning-making question, "If something were different, what would that mean?" That question could have many different contexts, the most important context being you. What would that mean about you as a person? For example, what does it mean about you that you're capable of being more confident, less depressed, or whatever the case may be? It means you have the potential to become what you desire. It means that outcome can be present in your life.

We've spent a good amount of time in this book establishing the stance that there is no such thing as a problem. You need to fully embrace that perspective to be difference-led and meaning-focused. Yes, you will face obstacles as you pursue your desired outcome, but those obstacles are going to teach you things—how to change your strategy or how to become stronger, for example.

To be difference-led, you need to think, *What would be different if I actually got what I wanted?* Beyond that, on every step of the journey, you should also think, *When I encounter an obstacle, I need to view that obstacle differently.* Instead of a problem, you view it as something that's going to help you be successful in the end.

On perfecting the design for the electric incandescent light bulb, Thomas Edison famously said, "I have not failed. I've just found 10,000 ways that won't work."[2]

He didn't look at each failure and say, "I didn't get it." He said, in essence, "I didn't get it *yet*." He needed to learn to do something differently in the process. Those experiences were learning opportunities he embraced, which he made clear in another of his famous quotes: "I never did a day's work in my life, it was all fun."[3]

How can you be like Thomas Edison? How can you start to think about your journey and its meaning differently?

Let's say someone handed you a backpack filled with a million dollars. What you choose to do with that million dollars would be unique to you. If it were mine, maybe I'd put it in the bank, save most of it for my kids to go to college, and perhaps take my wife to Italy, where she's always wanted to travel. What that money represents to me is the difference. It's the meaning. It would mean security for and serenity with those I love.

If Elliott got a million dollars, maybe he'd buy his favorite car and a nice watch for his mom. He would give a very different meaning to that same million dollars. For him, that million dollars might mean the ability to share joy and the opportunity to experience something he never thought possible.

What each of us would do with a million dollars represents the first level of difference that I defined a moment ago. You get to the second level of difference by asking, "What difference would it make?" In my case, I'd ask myself, "What difference would it make to be able to take my wife on a trip to Italy?" In Elliott's case, he'd ask himself, "What difference would it make to finally get the car I've wanted my whole life?"

Finally, the third level of difference is reached when you ask, "What would it mean?" What would it mean to me as I'm walking with my wife through Italy? What would it mean to Elliott to know he's finally arrived a place in his life where he can afford a luxury car?

Learn to think beyond "I want something" or "I want to become something." That kind of thinking doesn't get you very far. But when you think about the difference you want, the meaning you want, you give yourself the greatest odds at becoming or achieving what you desire. You'll know the reasons, the importance, and the value of what you want. You'll view obstacles differently because your motivation, your vision, and your "why" will be clear.

MAKING "LOVE" THE DIFFERENCE

Diving Deep with Elliott

Doing things from the place of difference is so important, and for Adam and me, that difference was love. We truly loved one another and loved working together, and for that reason, ambition stopped mattering. We never talked about how to make a ton of money or how to become famous. We just focused on wanting to work more together and how to impact more people. One day we hoped to do so full time. If there was any plan, that was the meat of it.

Because we were focused on difference, we endured hardships we wouldn't have been able to do otherwise. If the difference isn't meaningful, you quit. You give up on the journey. But the difference was so meaningful and impactful to us that we endured many hardships, both personally and professionally.

For over a decade, we kept finding ways to meet and continue to work on projects, and then in April 2020, I called Adam and said, "Something has happened."

"What?" he said.

"We've made $15,000," I replied.

He asked how, and I explained I'd figured out how to make some improvements with the online courses we were teaching. "I don't know if it's going to continue," I said, "but something's definitely happening."

Two weeks later, I called Adam again. "It's still happening. I don't know if it's going to continue, but it is still happening."

By the end of May, we had made over $100,000 in one month, and that momentum continued to grow. Our aim remained the same. Our difference remained love. And when the payoff came, our focus remained on the difference.

We weren't the only ones to have profitable years in 2020. Even though the whole world was dealing with COVID-19, the upside was that everyone went online, so we had more access to people. But not all who prospered in 2020 continued to do so afterward. Most of them spent their money on mere things. They upsized their homes, bought jewelry for their partners . . . they just bought stuff frivolously. But I decided to use my assets to buy Adam's time because that's ultimately what we wanted all along, to spend more time together. I focused on the difference that money could make in our lives toward what we desired most.

By buying Adam's time, I paid him a salary that allowed him to resign at the university, and I worked hard to get us a great health insurance package—a necessity for him and his family.

Now that the world is past the emergency stage of COVID-19, online sales are very different. Most businesses that thrived during the pandemic are struggling or closing, but we are not because I didn't waste the money on things. Instead, I put structure for our business in place. Now I can say to Adam, "We need you to do a webinar next week," and he doesn't reply, "I can't because I have a meeting at the university." Adam and I can now work together full-time, and in consequence, the impact we make is even greater.

From the very beginning of our working relationship, which developed into a deep friendship, the difference we focused on—love for each other and a shared love for helping others—has kept us on the journey. It kept us from quitting.

One of my favorite poems is "Footprints," which has many versions and many claims to its authorship. But the one I read—the one that had the most meaning to me—was printed on a poster that hung on my girlfriend's dorm room wall. This was back in college when I was at a really low point in my life.

"Footprints" is about a dream someone has of walking along the beach with the Lord while scenes from that person's life flash by. During the hardest times of life, only one pair of footprints appears in the sand. The person questions the Lord about this: "Why, when I needed you most, have you not been there for me?" The Lord replies, "My precious child, I love you and would never leave you. During your times of trial and suffering, when you see only one set of footprints, it was then that I carried you."

I burst into tears when I read the last part. It definitely hit home. There are times when life is just too hard and you can't do it on your own. The weight is too heavy. You need someone to carry you. During my career, Adam has been that person for me. More than once I've had to call him and say, "Adam, the weight is too heavy today. I cannot do this."

And the gift he would give is how he'd reply, without letting me off the hook, "Okay, Elliott. I'll share the load."

Then I could do it. I wouldn't get off the phone, instantly cured of my exhaustion and stress, but I'd think, *All right. I can keep going one more day.*

Without that kind of love, that kind of difference, Adam and I wouldn't have continued our solution focused work together. We wouldn't have had a million-dollar year in 2020. We would have given up long ago.

Sometimes life gets so heavy that you have to acknowledge, "I can't carry the weight today." Find people in your life that will inspire you, that will help you share the burden.

EVERYONE HAS A DIFFERENCE MAKER IN THEIR LIVES

A Closer Look with Adam

When people look at the relationship that Elliott and I have, they often express a wish to gain a similar relationship in their lives. "How did you find your Elliott?" they ask, or in Elliott's case, "How did you find your Adam?" We believe everyone has an Adam or an Elliott, if they look hard enough and if they're willing to put in the work to nurture that relationship.

We have an acquaintance who is jealous of our friendship, and Elliott gave her some advice one day that she should start talking to another woman, a mutual acquaintance, to get to know her better. That was offensive to her because she'd taught this woman Solution Focused Brief Therapy before and had also been her supervisor. Those reasons prevented her from being willing to form a friendship. Thankfully, none of that mattered to Elliott and me in the beginning.

Elliott could have easily said to me, "You're not even in private practice, and you don't know how to get on a stage. I don't want to work with you or know you better." And I could have dismissed him because I had a Ph.D. and worked at a university. But we didn't let those reasons become obstacles. We didn't care about how we could climb the political ladder together.

We didn't become friends right after we had that pivotal conversation in Malmo, Sweden. We didn't even recognize we could have fun together yet. What we did realize is that we had something in common, despite our differences. We found connection in how we viewed solution focused thought, which surprised us because we believed we were isolated in our opinions. We decided to keep in touch weekly, and the connection between us grew. When obstacles came, we depended on each other for support. Those experiences pushed to a different and deeper level of closeness, openness, and appreciation.

Human beings spend a lot of energy trying to figure out how to overcome differences with each other. But to Elliott and me, overcoming differences isn't what's important. *Accepting* differences is. He totally accepts me. I totally accept him. And because we've done that from the beginning, our work relationship shifted and became more personal. He started coming to my house and spending time with my family.

Elliott and I always think we're as close as we could possibly be as friends, but because of new and challenging situations we live through, we continue to become even closer, and we are constantly surprised that we keep getting closer. It happens as we unceasingly accept one another and depend on each other's differences.

He makes fun of me and says I have no swagger, but he never asks me to change the way I dress. He never asks me to change anything about myself. He just says, "That's exactly who you are, and it's okay. I like you because of that."

Over the years, as someone would be discriminatory to Elliott, or he'd call me and say he couldn't carry the weight any longer, or Becca would go through cancer, we would rely on each other even more.

If all we had done was focus on our problems, we would have said, like many people do, "Man, you know what? Life is just too hard. I've got to cut some things from my plate, and our friendship is one of those things." If Elliott and I had done that, we wouldn't have the reward that our relationship is today.

We didn't quit when difficulties came along the way. We carried each other through the hard times. We chose to think and act differently, and we chose to persevere.

Our relationship wouldn't have continued past that first time we got to know each other in Malmo, Sweden, without a lot of intention. We had no idea how successful a team we would be or how far our impact would spread. What we wanted was the deepest level of difference, which for us was connection, love, acceptance, appreciation, and innovation in our field. And by nourishing those things, even when life presented significant obstacles, the meaningfulness of our relationship expanded well beyond our expectations. And it continues to do so.

Be on the lookout for when you have a satisfying interaction with someone. Consider doing something to further that interaction. How can you meet up with or talk with that person again? Nourish the seed of that relationship and see if it's worth nourishing more. Surround yourself with people who make you feel good, people who appreciate what you have to say, people who respect you and are open to understand your point of view. When you do form a valuable relationship, don't cast it away when the inevitable obstacles arise. Lean on that relationship, and do the same for others when they need to lean on you.

APPRECIATING PEOPLE WHO ARE DIFFERENT

A Closer Look with Adam

Amid all that Elliott and I had in common to begin with, as far as viewpoints on solution focused thought we had many differences. We still do. We are two remarkably different people. I have skills and abilities that he doesn't have—that he never wants to develop, for that matter—and he has an equal number of skills and abilities.

As Elliott puts it, "At times, you're Batman and I'm Robin, and at other times, I'm Batman and you're Robin."

We're both clear on who we are and what we bring to this relationship, and we aren't threatened by each other's differences. We're grateful for them. When he shines, I sit back and relish in his ability to shine. And when I shine, he sits back, completely happy to let me have my moment in the spotlight.

There's value in surrounding yourself with people who are different from you, who see things differently, who esteem different things, but who also complement you. Elliott pushed me to do the things I wouldn't have chosen to do on my own, but those things ended up making me better.

One was being able to stand in front of the camera. I had to work hard to gain the knowledge I needed in such a clear way so that, when placed in front of a camera, I could be confident with everything I needed to teach.

It's easy to overlook what others see in us. Elliott thought I had enough knowledge to be on camera, but I didn't think so until I learned for myself what he saw in me.

Elliott and I have other kinds of differences. We have very different backgrounds and perspectives on culture and society, but we both respect each other's point of view. At times when we don't agree, we reach a place of understanding. We allow each other to hold our different perspectives and maintain that both can be accurate. It's not our responsibility to change those viewpoints.

We don't have an expectation of "you have to be exactly like me" or "you need to see things the way I do." You can be totally different, and I appreciate your difference.

We actually disagree a lot. Elliott's lived experience is vastly different from my lived experience, so we frequently have conversations filled with conflict as we try to understand each other. But there is never hate, judgment, or disrespect between us. Instead, we navigate these sensitive topics through love and appreciation, which leads to profound insights and deeper connection.

Remember, calmness and conflict can coexist, and in that calmness, we feel free to say whatever we want to each other. When we don't reach agreement, we still understand where the other person is coming from, so we ultimately arrive at a place of peace.

When people engage in conflict, they often expect resolution to mean agreement. But resolution just means truly acknowledging the other person. People want to be heard.

Although Elliott and I have many different perspectives, we share desired outcomes in our friendship and our work. Think of perspectives like the various places people are coming from on a map. Those places have different vantage points, and the roads traveled will be different, but people can still reach a common destination.

Questions to Ask Yourself about Being Difference-Led

- What changes/successes am I waiting for before I am willing to change my perspective?
- What is one difference I can start paying attention to that will start the change process in my life?
- How would noticing differences change my life?
- What would it mean about me if I could start to notice differences that were small or significant?
- What signs would let me know that I was in a relationship (friendship, partnership, or romantic) with a person who supported me and helped me be the best version of myself?

CHAPTER 6

BE OUTCOME-LED

THE POWER OF HOPE

A Closer Look with Adam

In addition to solution focused thought being difference-led, it's also outcome-led. When we speak of outcomes, what we mean is the desired outcome you want to achieve. We also call this your best hope. Consequently, solution focused thought is also hope-led. What will be different—what transformation will occur—if you live consistently with your best hope?

Transformation happens when hope takes root and continues to flourish. Hope is that driver of change. Hope is healing, and that healing is measurable and tangible on the human brain. Trauma, on the other hand, is destructive.

When people experience trauma, their hippocampus is impacted and has a difficult time distinguishing between past, present, and future. Consequently, when they experience a flashback, they can't determine whether their trauma is currently happening or if it happened in the past. To make matters worse, their amygdala starts flooding the brain with fear, worry, and stress.

Hope is the remedy. It's dynamic on the brain, which then becomes good at distinguishing between past, present, and future. Distinguishing the future, in turn, enables people to open their minds to new possibilities simply because the amygdala is now flooding the hippocampus with hope, optimism, and joy.

Belief is powerful. When people believe in themselves, they become capable of anything. Even on your hardest days, when it might be difficult to believe in yourself, what would let you know that hope was still present?

Hope can be derived by making a contrast from the worst, the most painful, and the most difficult challenge to the most hopeful outcome.

Be diligent about creating thoughts that are hope-filled. Talk to yourself in a hope-filled way. Extend that gift of hope-filled conversations to others as well. That's how hope grows and helps you become an agent of change. Once you discipline yourself to implement hopeful thoughts and language, you'll transform into a hope-filled person who can achieve your desired outcome.

THE MOST LOVING WALK AROUND THE BLOCK

Diving Deep with Elliott

Adam shared a story earlier about the heart attack his mom had when he was young. That story reinforces our stance that there are no problems, only lessons. Is Adam glad his mom had a heart attack? No, he didn't want that to happen. But something came from it that he needed.

I've mentioned many times now how strong Adam is. I have not seen him shaken much over the several years I've known him. But one of those times was after Becca's first chemotherapy treatment. For days afterward she was in serious pain, and there were even a few times she lay crying in a fetal position. "There's nothing I can do," Adam confessed to me on the phone. "I just have to watch this, and it's killing me." He never talks like that.

I'd continue to check in with him often over the next few months. "How's it going?" I'd ask.

"Terrible," he'd say. Basically, chemo was just wrecking Becca. Another time we were talking, he told me, dejected, "The doctor says Becca now has to exercise. She has to move, even though she feels like crap."

He continued to give me updates over the next several weeks. "Well, Becca walked from the front door to the mailbox and back," he'd say. "It's so hard because she's usually so energetic, and now it takes everything in her just to go to the mailbox and back."

During another update, I'd hear, "It's going a bit better. Becca now goes from the front door to the stop sign at the end of the block and back."

We eventually reached the point where I could come visit for the first time since all Becca's cancer treatments had started. During that visit, Adam told me, "It's time for Becca's daily walk. Do you want to come?"

"Sure," I said.

We went on a walk from the front door to the stop sign, and during that walk Adam and I delved deep into a meaningful conversation, which we're known to do. We often find ourselves talking about religion, social justice, or our solution focused therapy work. I don't remember the content of this conversation, but Becca was just quietly listening and walking with us. When we got to the stop sign, which had always been her turning point to go back home, she said, "I think I can keep going."

We replied, "You sure? We can turn around."

"No, no," she insisted. "I can keep going."

On this route in Adam's neighborhood, there's a point of no return. Once you pass that stop sign, you've gone over halfway, so you just have to finish going around the circle of their block to get back home again.

This specific walk was on a warm day in Georgia, and the route was up and down a few hills in their neighborhood. Despite that, Becca told us, "I can keep going." She didn't let us talk her out of it.

We kept walking and finally returned to their house. It was then it became clear to me that the only reason Becca had done what she did—walk past the stop sign and around the whole block—is because she loves Adam and likes to see him happy.

Adam, deep in a conversation with me, was a version of himself she doesn't always get to see because I don't live in Atlanta. To her, it was a better choice to suffer so that he could stay in that moment and talk to his best friend a little while longer. That must have come at a big sacrifice to Becca with her physical strength and health. Talk about an act of love.

I want people to know that fear, hate, anger, and revenge are not as powerful a motivator as love. I wouldn't know that to the extent I do if I didn't know Adam and Becca. If I hadn't experienced love first from him and then her, and witnessed it in the way they both walk through the world together, I wouldn't know the power of love as deeply as I do.

Now I pay attention differently to the way I walk through the world. I share love more fully and intentionally. I share it the way it's been given to me from Adam and Becca.

Who has shown you exceptional love in your life? How has that changed you? How have you used love as a motivator to help you accomplish difficult things?

DISCOVERING YOUR PURPOSE

A Closer Look with Adam

Once you understand your purpose in life, it will guide everything else you do, including moving toward the desired success you want to achieve. However, if you choose a desired outcome that isn't in line with your purpose, it will cause you grief in the end.

Elliott and I have a mutual acquaintance who is a very accomplished musician. She loves to play the piano, can compose anything on the piano, and received a degree in music. But since then, she has switched to studying psychotherapy—a field Elliott and I love—but she hates. She was thriving when she was a pianist, and now she's struggling that she isn't.

If you asked her what her desired outcome is today, she would answer, "To become a well-known single-session therapist." But she's struggling mightily and can't finish her degree—in my opinion because it's not in line with her purpose. If she were to go back to what was driving her to be a musician before, she would surely find a useful form of motivation that might put her on a new track.

So how do you discover your purpose? For me, since I'm a very religious person, I find my purpose when I ask, "What am I here on earth to do?" or in other words, "What does God intend for me to do with my skills?" Other people may define their purpose through honest internal assessment. They can ask themselves questions like "What brings me joy? When I feel like I'm living to my fullest, what am I doing? How am I living my life? What choices am I making?"

To answer those questions, you have to know yourself well enough to understand what *does* bring you joy rather than what only brings you fleeting happiness. You have to distinguish between those two and choose what brings you the greatest joy.

Once you know what brings you joy—what you're here on earth to accomplish—that should then influence your desired outcome. Ask yourself, "If I live according to my purpose, how does that translate to what I need to achieve or become?"

Your purpose therefore impacts your desired outcome. You can have desired successes that are out of line with your purpose, but your life will go better when they align.

Your desired outcome in life may change, but your purpose does not move. My individual purpose is eternal happiness with my family—being the best version of myself for them so we can ultimately achieve that level of happiness together—and that does not move. Maybe this year, to achieve that greater purpose, I might say, "I'm going to start running." Next year, I could say, "I'm going to address my mental health." The year after that, I might say, "I'm going to pick up a new hobby." The varying outcomes still build to my greater purpose. The pathway and pieces may move and shift, but the purpose stays the same.

I'm also aware of goodness, and I've been given goodness abundantly, so I have an outward purpose as well, one of spreading goodness—a purpose I share with Elliott. We want to change the world through love. We feel responsible to spread love, to share love, to teach love. Our outcomes toward that end shift through our educational efforts, among other things, but our compass is always directed toward love. Love has the power to completely change people's lives.

ELLIOTT'S 1,004TH YOUTUBE VIDEO

A Closer Look with Adam

Elliott started making videos for his YouTube channel in 2016. As he built his platform there, he never told me things like, "I hope I get on television doing this" or "I hope someone important watches this." He just enjoyed making videos and creating good and authentic content. It was the only part of the process he could control.

It didn't matter to him if only 10 people viewed each video or if 100 did. He didn't worry about the "thumbs-up" he accumulated. He simply wanted to tell his truth and live with the results.

In the business world and in Hollywood, people often ask Elliott, "How did you get discovered?" He tells them the same thing: "I was discovered when I put my 1,004th video on my YouTube channel." That's when a notable person contacted him about a TV contract as well as other opportunities.

To the people pursuing the dream that Elliott is now living, I ask, "Are you willing to make 1,000 videos when your only motivator is enjoying telling your truth?" Or are fame and fortune your motivators? If so, how will you remain happy over such a long journey to your outcome? Will you stick to your journey, or will it get further and further away from you? And if you do make it through your journey, how will you be satisfied once you achieve your outcome if you don't truly enjoy what you're doing?

Elliott found joy sharing with others all the profound things he and I had been researching and articulating each day about solution focused living. He wanted others to learn those truths as well. That's what excited him, not if or how the video would go on to benefit himself.

When Elliott was discovered by Hollywood, it wasn't just because he'd played a numbers game and the odds were that his time was due. Instead, over the course of a thousand videos, the quality of his videos improved. The content grew deeper. His ability to communicate became clearer. He started lighting his videos differently. He eventually hired a cameraman. Throughout his journey, there was a learning process.

Going back to the importance of how you view differences, Elliott looked at his obstacles differently. He didn't think, *Man, my 556th video didn't go big.* He thought instead, *What did I learn from video 556 that I need to make sure I implement with video 557?* He consistently asked himself, *What do I do to maximize this moment?*

When you maximize moments on your own journey, they will lead you toward your dream. In the process, you will learn and grow. Maybe your dream will change. Maybe you'll decide you want a different outcome along the way. But in the meantime, your happiness won't be contingent on your destination.

Elliott maximized each moment and found happiness during the process. He got better at what he was doing, and that improvement was what ultimately helped him get discovered.

It's okay to have a dream, but don't let your happiness depend on accomplishing it. Learn to love the journey. Find joy in the present and on your path to your desired outcome.

HAVING LOVING EYES

Diving Deep with Elliott

When I'm with Adam's family, they do something that makes me very uncomfortable. After they dish up their food, Adam will pick one of his family members to say a prayer to bless the meal. That makes me uncomfortable because praying out loud is not part of my world. I pray, but I've never done so aloud. Praying is very private for me. There have been a few times where Adam has called on me to say the dinner prayer, and I immediately reply, "Nope." One day I hope to have the courage to pray aloud in front of the Froerers because they're like family to me.

When that day comes, if every single Froerer, from little Juju up to Becca and Adam, stared at me with judgment, anticipating that I'm going to mess up, I would actually feel that negativity. It would reduce my likelihood of success. But if Adam's family looked at me with love and support, even if I stumbled, it would increase my likelihood of success. I call this kind of support, belief, love, and nonjudgment "loving eyes." You can literally feel the energy that loving eyes provides.

In addition to having loving eyes for other people, you can have loving eyes for yourself. For example, you can look in the mirror and say, "All right, I gained a few pounds recently, but I did just go through the holidays, and that's okay because I can also lose a few pounds." You don't have to beat yourself up for having gained some weight.

Loving eyes has also helped me have grace for myself with what I've been able to achieve in life. I am someone who has done all the work to earn a Ph.D., except I never wrote my dissertation. Later, I started another Ph.D., but got delayed when I signed my TV deal. Many other professionals in my field have obtained a Ph.D., so it would be easy for me to be hard on myself for not doing the same thing. But instead, I can look at myself with loving eyes and think, *I'm not defined by whether I complete this Ph.D. Perhaps God doesn't have it in the cards for me, and that's okay.*

People have a tendency to look at themselves through the lens of failure. They beat themselves up for those failures, even if they're micro failures, like not getting through their daily to-do lists. They also beat themselves up for major failures, like relapsing after being sober after several months.

Instead of all this beating up, it's important to find loving eyes for yourself. Train your brain to say, "You know, I relapsed last night. I've been through a lot lately. It's been tough. I had a weak moment, and I had a beer. I can forgive myself, stop drinking, and start the clock all over again." Likewise, in the other scenario, you can look at your unfinished to-do list and say, "I intended to accomplish more, but today got away from me. That's okay because I am superhuman."

I genuinely believe I am superhuman. I believe Adam is superhuman. And I believe each of you is superhuman. There are some days where you're going to be super and other days where you're going to be human. It's so valuable to channel your ability to look at yourself through the lens of love and say, "You know, it's okay that today I was human without the super."

As I write this, I am sitting in a mess of an office. I can't even tell you how many times I've been trying to clean this place up and turn into more of a studio with a cooler Zoom background for all my online meetings and social media videos. But I'm on a lot of planes these days, and sometimes I wake up and I'm just too tired. I have a million other things to do. It's okay for me to like myself while I'm failing.

People have a tendency to think, *When I see evidence of my failing, that means I'm a failure.* They don't realize we are all simultaneously successes and failures. None of us does everything we intend to do all the time, and none of us is ever doing nothing. At the same time, we produce evidence of wild success and evidence that we're human.

The power of loving eyes is significant. I have seen this as a practicing psychotherapist when working with clients as well as in my personal life. I have seen this when I look at myself and forgive myself for past mistakes. I am confident that learning to look at the world through loving eyes is how you change the world, and looking at yourself with the same loving eyes is how you change yourself.

LOVING EYES ON GOOD DAYS AND BAD DAYS

A Closer Look with Adam

Being outcome-led gives you a big-picture perspective on where you're trying to get to and who you want to become. It's a way to ask yourself daily, "Am I consistently moving in that direction in my life?"

You'll have superhuman days of success where you say, "Wow, today I had great momentum toward becoming the long-view version of my best self." You'll also stumble across days where you take a step backward, but you can still view yourself with loving eyes and say, "It's all right. Overall, I'm still moving in the direction I want to be moving."

Loving eyes makes the good days worth celebrating because they're consistent with the outcome you're hoping for, and loving eyes also gives you a perspective of grace on the bad days. Loving eyes allows you to say, "Okay, I fell down today, but I can still find kindness and understanding for myself."

It's also beneficial to look outward for more help with loving eyes. Ask yourself, "Who can I surround myself with that will look at me with those loving eyes? Who's going to be supportive of me? Who's going to lift me up? Who's going to care? Who's going to say, 'Get back up and try again?' Who's going to know I'm capable of being who I want to be?"

The low moments in life are just as important as the high ones because they teach you lessons about things you need to learn in order to obtain your outcome and become the best version of yourself. If all you experienced was success after success, you'd begin to take them for granted. You wouldn't understand the magnitude of who you're becoming. Likewise, if you never fell down, you'd never learn to think ahead and be stronger. You'd never say, "I'm surely going to encounter whatever just tripped me up again. What do I need to do to fortify myself against it so next time it's easier to overcome, or so that next time I can protect myself, or so next time I don't fall as far?"

Loving eyes are just as much about appreciating greatness as they are learning from your failures and mistakes.

LOVING EYES ARE RECIPROCAL

Diving Deep with Elliott

Adam's youngest daughter's given name is Julia, and several years ago, when I started coming by his house more often, he asked her, "What would you like Elliott to call you?"

She answered, "Juju," a nickname that only her family uses.

Right then I knew she was in the Loving Eyes Camp for me.

It's important to surround yourself with supportive and caring people. This might sound impossible to some of you. You may be in a toxic relationship or feel like you're only getting opposition from those you're close to as you work toward your desired outcome. You could be reading this chapter and thinking, *Well, loving eyes sound great, but I don't have someone to give them to me.*

Here's the message we want to share with you: you'll find loving eyes if you put more effort into finding them, giving them, and paying closer attention. The reason people don't find loving eyes so easily is they expect them to come from the obvious sources, like your mom or dad, your partner, your supervisor, or the popular crowd. For me, loving eyes weren't supposed to come from some dude I met at a conference in Austin and later bumped into in Sweden. But that's exactly where I found loving eyes because that's how Adam came into my life.

How can you find loving eyes? How about you post something positive on Facebook and watch to see who cheers for you consistently. People with loving eyes raise their hands. Or volunteer somewhere and play a game with a kid. Kids just naturally love and care. You could get yourself a dog. You'll always be loved and accepted. What about that homeless person on the street? Give them $5 and start a conversation. While you're at the store, hold the door open for someone. Go to a hospital and say, "Point me toward the patients who haven't had visitors." Walk into those rooms and talk with those people. Be purposeful in kindness, and you'll start to notice when kindness is given in return. You'll begin to see yourself as the sort of person who can change another person's life.

At any point on your journey toward your best self, you may fall down and think, *I just don't feel like I've got it in me to try today. I've lost sight of the outcome I thought I had. I don't believe it anymore.* Those are times you can turn to someone else and ask, "Can you help me recapture it?"

Part of why you might have lost the perspective of "I don't have people with loving eyes in my life" is because you also have to give those loving eyes. You have to see them for yourself *and* others. If you go out of your way and take the time to give loving eyes to someone else—that homeless person or the patient in the hospital or the stranger walking in the door after you—you will, by nature, get loving eyes in return.

When I first got to know Adam, I found I was giving him the same thing he was giving me. We were seeing each other in a very similar light. That's how I was able to recognize his loving eyes. It was reciprocal.

Whatever you want, give that thing away and you'll get it back tenfold. Many religious traditions teach this. Christians say, "Love your neighbor as you love yourself," which often gets interpreted as, "I have to love myself, and then I have to love my neighbor like I love myself." But it just means love your neighbor, and then that love will come back to you. Only then will you begin to love yourself. In Buddhism, it's the concept of karma. You put out what you want to get back. They're both expressing the same thing: give goodness first, and then you'll get it in return. Live a life of love, and love will come back to you.

A SEA OF GRAY HONDA CIVICS

A Closer Look with Adam

When you start giving loving eyes to others, your senses become primed to noticing loving eyes in return. It's like when you buy a new car and then notice that same car on the road more often. Your senses become more aware of it.

Elliott likes to say I'm a maniac behind the wheel of a car. He also says I have a mischievous streak. I disagree, but I'll tell you a story and let you judge for yourself.

One day while Elliott was in Atlanta where I live, he needed to return his rental car to the airport and get a ride back to my house. I drove there in my own car while he followed me in his rental car. Or at least he tried to follow me.

According to Elliott, once I got on the highway, I started driving as if I'd just robbed a bank. "Like a loon," he later told me.

"More like proficient," I'd argued. Predictably, Elliott lost me in the sea of cars.

From my perspective, once I'd gotten on the highway and started driving as fast as I normally do, I noticed Elliott wasn't paying close attention. He started checking his phone and texting, and in the process, he began slowing down.

I wasn't waiting for him, I decided. He knew how to find his way to the airport. I kept driving the way I do—not like a maniac, I assure you, but like a reasonable and responsible person—and my wife Becca who was in the car with me, said, "You need to slow down. Elliott can't keep track of you."

"Nope," I replied. "If he's on his phone, it's his own fault. He can catch up if he wants."

At some point, Elliott finally decided to catch up with me. This turned out to be more difficult than he'd anticipated. I drive a Honda Civic because I like tiny cars, and as Elliott was on the lookout, apparently every car on the highway turned into a gray Honda Civic.

According to his highly dramatic retelling of this event, he had to go "a thousand miles an hour" to catch up with me. Every time he pulled up beside a gray Honda Civic, he'd squint into that car to see who was driving, and it would be anyone but me. As he kept pulling up to gray Honda Civics and peering into windows, he looked like a bona fide creeper—and it may have been very amusing.

Finally, he pulled up beside *my* gray Honda Civic and made his squinty creeper face. I burst out laughing. Perhaps after that moment I *did* try to lose him on purpose, just so I could see him do it again.

My point in telling this story, other than giving you all a taste of the joys of being Elliott's friend, is that when you do something with intention, you notice that certain something more in your life. You become attuned to it. You realize that it was there the whole time.

When someone tells me, "There's nobody to look at me with loving eyes," I think, *Yes, there is. You've had that the whole time. And you can have even more of it.*

Having unconditional positive regard is important, but you have to be prepared to give it without expectation for it to return to you. If you do it with expectation, it becomes manipulation. Instead, love someone because you think he or she is a good person. Do it because it's a good thing to do. That's the only way genuine love reciprocates.

When you're loving, the world transforms into a more loving place. You receive love in return, and you're primed to notice that love. You realize it was there the whole time.

TRUSTING IN THE PERMANENCE OF YOUR DESIRED OUTCOME

Diving Deep with Elliott

Your transformation into the best version of yourself can become your new reality. People sometimes fear that everything they have gone through and worked so hard to achieve is just temporary. When you're no longer living in poverty, for example, you fear that your new state won't last. But it's important to believe it can endure because that thinking will change your actions. You'll avoid "mistakes of the poor," such as burning through windfalls of money because you haven't learned the mindset and skills to save and invest.

I am someone who had to work very hard to move myself upward socioeconomically. I'm not the richest man in the world, but I no longer live in poverty. There was a time in my life when I'd just spend excess money on more Air Jordans. I didn't trust in my increased income—I didn't know how to live in permanence with it—so I just bought things I wanted *now.* I eventually aged through that and learned from my "mistakes of the poor" and finally accepted who I had become was truly the new me.

People who struggle with addiction and then commit suicide are another example of those who don't believe their changed state is going to last. They think, "I can't be the nondrinker forever," and then when they relapse, they no longer see the point in living anymore. But the point is that they can be different now. The new version of themselves may relapse, but that doesn't mean they're back to square one as the old version of themselves.

Failure is part of whatever journey you're on. You can still be who you desire to be, and while you won't be that perfectly, you can be that permanently.

GIVING YOURSELF GRACE IN YOUR TRANSFORMATION

A Closer Look with Adam

Remember that change of any kind is initially uncomfortable. As part of your transformation into your best self, you're going to need time to settle into the new feeling and reality of it. Take getting married, for example. That's supposed to be a good change.

People expect to be overjoyed when they're first married and not experience any negative feelings or associations with it, when the reality they often overlook is that they're also giving up a sense of freedom, a sense of autonomy. They have to give up their own living space to join with someone else in their living space. And they're now accountable to that other person 24/7. All those things are big changes, and change is uncomfortable.

To use the example that Elliott mentioned of someone now living sober, that transformation can be uncomfortable. Perhaps after becoming sober, a man has gained a new job and a better place to live, but now he has the pressures and demands of a boss he didn't have before. Now he needs to hold himself together because other people will be watching him and waiting to see if he slips up. Now he has a more expensive rental payment because he's living in a nicer place. Now he has more things he can lose, like his job or his apartment or new relationships.

What isn't new to him, however, is how he's dealt with discomfort in the past, and he's managed that by drinking. So, although some things are changing for the better, he may not live consistently with the new version of himself and reverts to the version he does know, the version he's comfortable with, but then he regrets it.

Part of the concept of loving eyes is to give yourself some grace in your transformation. Sit for a minute in the inevitable discomfort. Let your mind, your body, and your experience catch up. Be patient and forgiving with yourself. Even as you deal with what looks like positive transformation, it comes with new expectations and new requirements, and you have to grow into that.

In the chapter about autonomy, we talked a little about how peace can coexist with discomfort, and as you learn to be the new you, you're going to run into that dichotomy. Peace is the absence of conflict or the absence of chaos or the presence of tranquility. Typically, you can only know peace after you've made it through a period of war. Peace is defined by its opposite.

Calmness, however, is a bit different, and I've learned to appreciate it even more than peace. You can think of it, in some ways, as a deeper level of peace—one you can control.

Calmness is an internal state. It's a feeling, an emotion. You can feel calm in the midst of chaos. If you're a mom and your children are arguing, for example, you can tell yourself that today you won't yell at them. During the chaos, you'll draw on the calmness within you and handle the situation differently. You might not be experiencing peace in that moment, but you can be calm.

Peace might be more of a long-term objective, but in the meantime you can have calmness. Perhaps all that calmness will culminate until you eventually achieve peace.

As you transform into the new you, be kind to yourself during your personal wars of discomfort. Know that peace will be realized at some point in your endeavor, and on the journey there you can give yourself grace and channel calmness.

Questions to Ask Yourself

- As I practice looking at myself with loving eyes, what is one or more thing(s) I notice this time that I have overlooked previously?
- Who in my life looks at me with the most loving eyes? What do they see in me that others may not see?
- Who in my life is most in need of my loving eyes? What is one thing I could to do help them know that my loving eyes truly see them? What difference would it make to them to interact with my loving eyes?
- What transformation would I most like to see within myself? What signs would I notice that would let me know I was moving in the direction of my desired transformation?
- What would it mean about me if I started noticing that I was moving in the direction of my desired transformation?

CHAPTER 7

PRESUPPOSE THE BEST IN YOURSELF AND OTHERS

THE "BAD" STUDENT

Diving Deep with Elliott

My previous battles with depression helped me develop the skill to presuppose the best in others and eventually myself. Growing up, I wished influential people had viewed me in the best light possible when in reality they viewed me in the worst.

During my high school years, I rarely did my homework. Consequently, my teachers and administrators determined I wasn't a good student or studious by nature. They labeled me as unintelligent, even though I scored high every time I took their intelligence tests. Despite that, I was still treated like a bad student and kept getting kicked out of class.

When I walked into my math classroom, my teacher would ask, "Elliott, do you have your homework?"

I would answer, "No."

He would say, "Go sit in the office."

I spent most of my freshman year doing math homework in the vice principal's office. I'm sure it wouldn't surprise you to learn that math never became my strong suit.

Instead of judging me, I wished someone would have presupposed the best in me, assumed I had a good reason, and asked, "Why don't you do your math homework?"

I would have answered, "Because my dad beats me up."

When he found out I hadn't done my math homework yet, he beat me, so I learned to tell lies. "I've already done my math homework," I'd say, only to have him beat me up for rushing through it. I learned to tell a different lie: "I'm going to do it later so I can focus." That didn't work either; he'd beat me for not taking it seriously. The only trick that worked was to not mention my math homework at all. And if I didn't do it, I just didn't do it.

I used to set my alarm clock for 2:00 in the morning because it was the safest time to do my homework. Everyone in the house was asleep by then. Sometimes I was able to wake up and work for one or two hours. Sometimes I accidentally slept through my alarm clock and didn't get any work done.

As an adult looking back now, I'm able to see that the person I've just described—a boy who was willing to wake up at 2 A.M. to do his homework—seems like a very studious person. Unfortunately, everyone treated me like I didn't respect homework or that I didn't take academics seriously.

I came to believe I was stupid because when enough people tell you you're dumb, you eventually believe it.

What helped me become the way I am now was wishing someone had looked at me with more perspective—like there was a justifiable reason for what was going on, like I actually had a strength instead of just a problem.

After all, I had found a way to protect myself from my father's beatings. True, it came at the cost of my high school academics, but I did find a way to keep myself safe.

How did I change from a being a C student in high school to an A student in college? I met a professor, Dr. Michael Ellison, who caused me to doubt my perceived truth about myself.

"You're a very good writer," he told me one day. "Where did you learn to write like that?"

I stared at him blankly, taken aback. "I didn't know I was a good writer."

He took me into his office and said, "Elliott, I have to be honest with you. The one part of my job I hate is grading papers. I feel like I'm reading the same papers over and over again. But there's something different about your papers. When I get to the end of them, I find myself wishing there was more. As someone who doesn't like grading, that's very rare for me."

I couldn't believe what I was hearing. Slowly, the fog of negativity in which I had viewed myself started to clear. When we finished speaking, I didn't walk out of my professor's office convinced of my own brilliance as a writer, but I did walk away doubting the reality that I was dumb.

As you learn to demonstrate that same level of faith in yourself, it's helpful to argue the negativity of your reality and view yourself in a new and kinder light. Think past your obstacles and ask yourself, "What strength is hiding within me? What am I overlooking about myself?" Train your brain to see yourself and others through a prism of strength.

For the record, I graduated college with a 4.0 GPA and later did the same while working toward my Ph.D. I trace the pivot point of my success back to my early college professor, who presupposed the best in me.

FIND THE HERO IN THE STORY

A Closer Look with Adam

Presuppositions are an important component of solution focused thought, so what exactly what does it mean? A presupposition is an assumption in which the truth of that assumption is taken for granted. In other words, before you know something, you suppose in advance that it's true. In solution focused thought, presuppositions are positive. We go out of our way to assume the best about ourselves and others, and in doing so, we help evoke change—the desired outcome we're seeking for ourselves and helping others to seek for themselves.

Maintaining the belief that people can overcome their obstacles and achieve their outcomes is presupposing in action. "Find the hero in the story" is our mantra. We want you to do the same. The better you become at allowing yourself to be amazed by people, the better you'll learn to be amazed by yourself. Practice this skill in your everyday life, even in simple moments such as watching TV, reading a book, or interacting with others on social media.

When Elliott was watching *Chopped*, an American TV cooking competition show, one of the competitors stood out to him. She was a vegan chef, and during one episode she was given meat that she was required to use in a recipe.

Staying true to her vegan lifestyle, she didn't taste the meat as she prepared it, but as a result she didn't know if her dish was seasoned well. She found a workaround.

After cooking the meat, she cut off a small piece and ran it over to one of the other chefs to ask if he would taste it for her. He did and told her it needed a little more salt. She added more and asked him to taste it again. This time he said it was perfect.

Elliott saw two heroes in that episode: the vegan who found a way to solve her problem and the contestant who helped her, even though he didn't gain any advantage by doing so.

Go through your life like this, looking for the heroes in people. Look for strengths in others when it's easier to see their problems.

Look for strengths in yourself. Write them down to help you remember them so it's easier to battle your obstacles.

MENTALLY HEALTHY PEOPLE OWN THEIR STRENGTHS

Diving Deep with Elliott

We are trained as human beings to restrain from bragging about ourselves. People often say to me, "When you were a kid, you were great at baseball."

My instinct is to reply, "Yeah, it was just my thing."

But the truth is that a lot of people can't hit a baseball. That's a skill. It's something I should own, just like I do with my other talents.

We want you to take credit for your own skills, and we challenge you to do that.

My favorite rapper is Jay-Z, and back in 2008, Jay-Z was the first hip-hop artist to headline the Glastonbury Festival in the U.K. A lot of people criticized the festival's organizers for featuring a rapper, and the loudest critic was former headliner Noel Gallagher, lead guitarist and co-lead singer of the band Oasis.

"I'm sorry, but Jay-Z? No chance," Noel complained. "Glastonbury has the tradition of guitar music . . . I'm not having hip-hop at Glastonbury. It's wrong."

Jay-Z addressed Noel's protests in an interview with the magazine *Bizarre*. "We have to respect each other's genre of music and move forward," he said. "I've never ever had a show that's caused this much of a stir, so I'm looking forward to it."

What Jay-Z went on to do at the Glastonbury Festival speaks volumes. He walked out on stage with a guitar strapped around him—an instrument he barely plays—and he opened his set with a performance of Oasis's hit song, "Wonderwall."

Some of the audience sang along. Most of them chanted Jay-Z's name.

"For those that didn't get the memo," the rapper shouted, "my name is Jay-Z, and I'm pretty f***ing awesome."

What makes people like Jay-Z so amazing is that they claim their strengths. As human beings, we are trained to claim our flaws instead, and then we're rewarded by people who tell us we're humble. But to be mentally healthy, you have to claim your zones of genius—and it isn't arrogant to do so.

If my friend asked me to fix his car and I answered, "Sure, I'm a pro at fixing cars," that would be arrogant because I can't even change a tire. I'm not skilled with my hands. Instead, I should say, "I don't think I'm the person you should be asking, but I can give you the names of people who might be able to help."

On the other hand, if my friend were to ask, "Are you any good at Solution Focused Brief Therapy?" I have every justification to answer, "Yeah, I'm pretty f***ing awesome." After all, SFBT is in the wheelhouse of things I do well. It's my zone of genius.

Confident people own their strengths. Likewise, mentally healthy people own their weaknesses. I'm fine to tell people, "I'm a very bad wrench turner, but I'm a good check writer." I'll gladly pay someone to fix my car, and I can do so without shame.

What is your own zone of genius? Every person has one, even if they're not using it for the best reasons. Train your brain to think in a new way. Learn to recognize your own brilliance. Own what you're awesome at and devalue what you're not. Focus on your skills and strengths.

BECOMING COMFORTABLE WITH PRIDE

A Closer Look with Adam

I grew up in a culture where humility was emphasized to the extreme. One of the detriments of emphasizing humility is it sometimes robs you of the ability to be confident or proud of who you are or to claim your greatness. Our intention for this book is to help you become the superhero you have the potential to be. But you may be resisting that label. You may think you could never acknowledge that about yourself. Like Elliott mentioned, human beings are trained to be humble.

Elliott and I have talked many times about our huge cultural differences in the ways we were taught to minimize ourselves, including our skin color, our religion, and our upbringings.

For example, in Black culture, African Americans are now taught to own their greatness because they have been minimized for hundreds of years. Be proud, be loud, they say. Take a look at the clothing and music of celebrities in Black culture. Everything is about "I'm the biggest. I'm the greatest. I have the most."

Likewise, Elliott doesn't shy away from publicly saying, "I'm the greatest solution focused psychotherapist that ever was." When that gets backlash, he wonders why people are mad at him.

I say, "It's because your audience is largely white and Christian. They're taught to be humble, and you're hitting on what they think humility is."

But I am learning to be different and become more like Elliott. It's taken me a decade to do so, but I now believe that if I want to be the best version of myself, I have to own that. I have to say, "Elliott and I have a partnership that no one else in this field has ever had before. We've been able to achieve things no one has achieved before."

Going back to the concept of loving eyes that we discussed in the previous chapter, people often interpret loving eyes as being quietly humble and grateful for what they have. But loving eyes also means you're willing to declare that you can do something nobody else can do.

Elliott had to grow into acknowledging greatness because somebody tore it away from him, whereas I had to grow into acknowledging greatness because my culture is one of humility. The only way we grew into greatness together is because I had to look at his culture and the way he reflects it and get past my instinct to recoil at how he owns his pride. I had to acknowledge that it's perfectly fine for him to declare his greatness in the way he does. And if that's okay for him, it must be okay for me as well.

Like I said, getting to this point took me a decade. Until then, whenever Elliott wanted to put my name in his e-mail newsletters or YouTube videos or tag me on social media, I resisted it. Recognition and pride made me uncomfortable.

If you're like I was, be patient with yourself as you learn to own your greatness. Tap into being outcome-led and honestly ask yourself: What version of myself do I want to be? What is my mission? What is my purpose? To answer those questions, you have to really know yourself.

What I know about myself is my purpose and Elliott's purpose are connected. We have things on this earth that we need to do together, things that neither one of us will achieve on our own. We want to change the world through love. We want people to look at race differently. We want people to look at what makes up meaningful relationships differently.

Knowing that outcome, that purpose, helps me move past discomfort with owning pride and greatness. I recognize that claiming my greatness actually keeps me in line with my shared purpose with Elliott. If it's okay for him to get on a stage and say, "If you do what Adam and I do, you can also achieve greatness," then it's okay for me to do the same. I'm able to get over my own insecurity to live according to who I am and who we are together.

What is wonderful about Elliott is that he believes and declares that not only is he a superhero but also that everyone else is a superhero too. It's not just self-praise; it's praise for all. That goes back to our stance of loving eyes. Loving eyes go both ways. They're equally applicable to you as they are to everyone else.

Elliott and I value our differences, and that has also helped each of us toward our shared purpose. I learn from him, appreciating how he owns the hero within himself, and he learns from me. Elliott has told me that some of the practices I incorporate in my life also make him uncomfortable, but he adopts them too because he knows they're in line with our desired outcome.

DECLARING YOUR TRUTH

Diving Deep with Elliott

Adam's youngest daughter, Juju, struggles with anxiety. Adam and his wife, Becca, have had to tell Juju countless times, "You can do it," whether that applied to a swim meet or a school project or a math test. My story is different. I heard that zero times growing up. When I was 10 years old and anxious about a test I had to take the next day, there was no one to tell me, "You can do it." I had to lie in bed stressing all night. The anxiety would make me late to school, I'd do poorly on the test, and then I'd come home and have my backside beaten.

Eventually, as more tests and other stressors came my way, I had to figure out a mechanism to get through them that wouldn't get me beaten again. I learned to tell myself, "You can do it."

Like Adam mentioned, sometimes when I publicly declare my own greatness, people get mad, and I wonder why. All I'm doing is talking myself through difficult things. I didn't lie in bed as a 10-year-old thinking, *I am better than everyone else.* I just had to say something to get myself up and get my shoes on.

If all people did was win, they would take winning for granted. Sometimes my win was that I got myself to school, and I had to do it coming from an empty house. There was no parent cheering me on, no one saying, "When you get home, we'll have ice cream and cookies to celebrate." When I woke up every morning, both of my parents had already left for work. Under the threat of being beaten later if I failed to get to school on time, I had to learn to get myself out of bed. When I managed to do that, I considered it a win, just like getting dressed and walking myself to school where also wins. I learned how to pat myself on the back.

My relationship with Adam has been very valuable over the years, especially as he's someone I can ask, "Am I right that I'm pretty good at this thing? I think I am." I can go a step further and ask, "Am I great at this? I think so, but is it true?" I'm not saying I'm great overall; I'm just saying I happen to be great at this one needle prick of a thing. I suck at so many other things, but I believe I'm the Michael Jordan of Solution Focused Brief Therapy.

Can you imagine if everyone on this planet could find the skill that they were the Michael Jordan of and then have the courage to live their life according to that greatness? So many problems would go away.

I'm lucky that I found the thing I'm the Michael Jordan of, and I'll be damned if anyone's going to say, "Stop declaring you're Michael Jordan."

"Well, come watch me dunk," I'll reply. If you watch me in my element, you'll see it too.

I'm not saying I'm the Michael Jordan of car repair or the Michael Jordan of research or the Michael Jordan of screen writing. But I am the Michael Jordan of solution focused living. I went through a lot to become that and to find the bravery to own it.

Remember the story I told you about the woman, Jackie, that I worked with who went out of her way to make my life miserable? During that time, I came home one day and complained about her to my aunt. "Why is she doing this? I just want to go to work and see my clients, but she's hating on me and getting others to hate on me too."

My aunt's reply to me was very wise: "The Bible says, 'No weapon that is formed against you shall prosper,' but it doesn't say there won't be any weapons formed against you."

Wow, that's so true, I thought. It made me consider how God had to deal with a lot more opposition than I ever would. He declared his greatness and said, "I'm the Messiah," and because he did, he was ultimately crucified. But if he hadn't declared that, he wouldn't have changed the world. He could have still gone about doing good and performing miracles under the radar, but he wouldn't have created world change without also saying, "I'm the Messiah."

Luckily, you and I don't have to face literal crucifixion, but my point is that we can't get through this life without weapons formed against us. When opposition comes, we have to decide what we're going to do about it. Will we let it derail us from our purpose, which will lead to making us miserable, or will we hold on to our truth, which will lead to joy and fulfillment?

We can't avoid the arrows in life, but we can focus on what brings us lasting happiness.

EXPECT OPPOSITION TO TRANSFORMATION

Diving Deep with Elliott

In this book, we're encouraging transformation, but you need to be warned that any time you try to make a change, you will encounter opposition. Adam likes to remind me that, by nature, people want to remain in homeostasis, a relatively stable internal environment. It takes a lot more effort and energy to move, to change, to convert, to transform.

It shouldn't be surprising, then, when you start to change, you will be met with resistance on every level. Within yourself, you'll experience a war against transformation. Beyond that, your family may question you: "Hold up a second. You are not *that*. You don't fit into our family in that way. You are *this*." In society, you'll also find resistance to change because you'll be upsetting the status quo.

I can barely remember a time in my life when I wasn't doing just that because transformation has been a part of my journey since I was a young child. I doubt many people realized something needed to change in their lives as early as I did.

The first time I had a thought that my life was screwed up was when I was seven years old and in the third grade. I lived in Walton, Massachusetts, at the time. Up until then I hadn't received a true report card in elementary school. Report cards were more like "Elliott sat in class quietly" rather than "Elliott got an A in math." My grades had been pretty mediocre, and then one day my report card changed, and I got all A's in English.

I was so excited to go home and tell my dad. When I handed him the report card, he glanced over it and said, "You speak English. This don't mean shit." And he threw the report card at me. As young as I was, I thought to myself, *I'm not sure this is good.*

That night I packed a bag and put it under my bed, planning to run away. I remember thinking, *I can't stay like this.* I didn't have any real wisdom. I didn't know one day I'd meet the Froerers and everything would be okay. All I knew was I needed to figure out something different. Different was important. I hadn't learned what was right yet, but I knew what I was experiencing was wrong.

When you're on your journey of transformation, some people are going to be triggered by it because you stoke the demons of their insecurity. That's what happened with my dad. And he wasn't the only one I've triggered because I don't mind telling people I'm the greatest at my skillset. Muhammad Ali did the same.

One of his famous quotes is, "I am the greatest. I said that even before I knew I was." He understood that to become the greatest, he had to first believe it to be true. To that end, he started declaring it to the world. He was extremely outcome-driven. I also want to be the greatest, which means I have to say it. I've had to learn to be unapologetic about my journey and to accept that it will trigger some people's insecurities.

At times in the past, when discrimination against me became too hard and I was too exhausted to go on, God showed up for me in the people he brought into my life. Again, that's why my favorite poem is "Footprints." People like Adam carried me when I didn't have the strength on my own.

Keep on the path. Keep to your purpose. Own your greatness. Be courageous in your willingness to change, even if it upsets the status quo. Be the difference that makes the world a better place.

SHINE BRIGHTER THAN YOU'VE EVER SHINED BEFORE

Diving Deep with Elliott

I have a tattoo on my arm that says, "Why not?" I got it to honor my uncle Jeffrey, who coined that phrase for me. He'd say things like, "Oh, your car got totaled? Well, I'll build you a new car! I'll be back!" If your reply was, "Wait, you can't just build a car! You've never done that before!" he'd answer, "Why can't I? Why not?"

"Why not?" is just the way he thought. He was someone who could do almost anything with his hands, and when he didn't know how, he figured it out.

He'd come back a few weeks later covered in sweat and grease, having just built you that car he promised. Now, maybe it wouldn't be pretty. Maybe you wouldn't like the color. Maybe it would make strange noises. But it would run and get you from place to place.

Adam has heard me say many times that I'm allergic to doubt. I learned that from my uncle. If you looked him in the eye, you'd see he had complete faith in his abilities. He wouldn't let any obstacle get in his way. He presupposed the best in himself.

I was teaching at an event in Denmark when I checked my Facebook and read one of my cousin's posts. It said, "My uncle passed away." Coincidentally, this cousin shared another mutual uncle with me, who had passed away the week before. I thought maybe he was just finding out about that.

The next morning, I woke up with a pit of worry in my stomach. *What if two uncles have passed away?* I thought. Troubled, I called my aunt and asked, "Is Uncle Jeffrey okay?"

"No," she said, her voice choked. "He had a heart attack and died."

My uncle Jeffrey and I were very close, so this news was completely devastating, and I found out just an hour before I was supposed to teach at a big event. I managed to get myself to the venue, but I couldn't rein in my emotions. I went for a walk, knowing I only had about 10 minutes to spare before I needed to be on stage. I couldn't stop crying. I wanted to call Adam, but with the time difference between Denmark and Georgia, it would have been 1:00 in the morning for him, so I called a mutual friend of ours, Chris Iveson, instead.

Chris is a well-known practitioner of Solution Focused Brief Therapy who lives in London, and he would be awake, I realized. I was sure he could help me find a way to get out of teaching, given my situation. He's 30 years older than I am and therefore 30 years more experienced as a lecturer.

"Chris, I'm in trouble," I said, and told him everything that was going on. "How do I tell people I have to cancel this event?" I wanted to know how to do this in a way that wouldn't end my career.

After listening to me, Chris said in his very British way, "Oh dear."

"What?" I said, not sure where he was headed with the conversation.

"Elliott, you're a bright, shining star," he continued. "And I'm sorry, but you're going to have to shine brighter than you've ever shined before because that's what your uncle would have wanted."

That was the exact opposite of what I wanted to hear. I wanted Chris to tell me how to cancel the event and fix my problem. I didn't believe in problems, but in this moment, I thought I had one. That's how low I was feeling. Instead, Chris inspired me to persevere.

I got off the phone still crying, but I knew he was right because my uncle was the "I can do it" man, the person who taught me "Why not?" He wouldn't have wanted me to give up.

I got on stage, tears streaming down my face, and said, "Look, we have a two-day training ahead of us, and I'm going to give it my very best, but here's what I'm going through in my life. My uncle just passed away, and I'm in complete shock. I don't know what to do with myself. So, during the breaks, when you usually come up and ask me to sign books and take pictures, you might notice I'm off doing my own thing instead. Please just give me some space. I'm not being aloof or arrogant. I'm just really struggling."

For those two days, the attendees and I cried together. We also learned together. Chris was a real friend, and because he presupposed the best in me, he didn't give me what I wanted; he gave me what I needed.

Adam is also a real friend. I can't tell you how many times he gave me what I needed and not what I wanted. Likewise, I'm quite confident I haven't always been what Adam wanted, but I've always been what he needed.

Presuppose the best in yourself. Believe in the philosophy of "Why not?" Why can't you be the best version of yourself? Why can't you accomplish your desired outcome? During times you need a boost, find people who will push you by loving you, who will presuppose the best in you, who know you're a bright shining star and will help you keep shining.

Questions to Ask Yourself

- What are my true strengths?
- What can I be really proud of about myself?
- Am I someone who tries to avoid being proud of myself? If so, do I want to continue to live with this belief?
- What opposition might I encounter in pursuit of my desired outcome? What plans can I put in place now to help me be prepared to overcome that opposition?
- What would it mean about me if I were prepared to overcome opposition?

CHAPTER 8

TRUST YOUR CAPABILITY AND OTHERS'

NO ONE'S LIFE IS PERFECT

Diving Deep with Elliott

My favorite song is "God Did" by DJ Khaled. The song features many rappers. One of those rappers is Jay-Z, who references another rapper named Meek Mill, who went to jail when he was 19 for something stupid and was given an unjust and heavy-handed sentence, considering the crime. Jay-Z paid a huge amount of money to get him an attorney who got him out of jail and more recently got him pardoned.

Responding to the verse that he and Jay-Z could never beef, Meek Mill tweeted, "Never!!!!!!" and "GOD ALWAYS DID" because of the role that Jay-Z played in his life.[1]

I think about Adam in a similar way. If somebody called me and said Adam was talking behind my back, I'd reply, "I'm sure he has a good reason." You couldn't make me beef with Adam because of the role he's played in my life and the loving eyes he's always had for me.

As much as I absolutely adore him, however, Adam is the kind of person that I would have struggled to be around growing up, not because of anything related to him but because I wasn't programmed to think of myself with loving eyes due to my abusive childhood.

When I looked at people like Adam, my brain translated their lives as being perfect. I'd think, *They won the life lottery, and I lost it.*

One of the ways I've found healing on my journey is discovering flaws with Adam. I don't mean that I was on the lookout for what's wrong with him. I mean I started to recognize things I could do that he couldn't.

I'm not good at detailed things like Adam is, for example. He's excellent at dotting the i's and crossing the t's in life. But I'm great at big-picture things, like getting on stage in front of a large crowd and having an entrepreneurial mindset. It's been huge for me to see I have strengths that he lacks.

Going into adulthood, I knew I had capability, but I didn't know I had skills that other people couldn't easily replicate. I figured anything I could do another person could also do. But in my partnership with Adam because our skillsets are so complementary, it has been valuable to me to realize that there are also things I bring to this table.

I mention all this because, number one, a lot of people had childhoods like mine where they weren't praised. We developed coping skills to get through life, but we also have scars. And, number two, I hope more people can be like Adam, who had zero defensiveness whenever I'd have a realization and say things to him like, "You're not at good as big-picture things as I am, are you?"

He'd respond, "Yeah, you're right."

That allowed me to sit in the space of "Okay, that's my thing then. Got it." In other words, that allowed me to embrace my strengths.

I can't do research like Adam, but I can get a bigger audience to read his research than he could on his own. Most people won't admit to their flaws or their shortcomings like that. In arrogance, they would have said to me, "Well, I *could* get a bigger audience. I just don't want to." But Adam is humble in owning both his flaws and his strengths. He has no problem saying, "Doing that is your skillset, Elliott, not mine. I appreciate it and value it."

Having loving eyes for yourself is an ability that some people like me have to heal into. In order to do that, I had to have the courage to say vulnerable things to Adam, and if he'd handled them differently, it would have hindered if not stopped me from my healing. But because he reinforced my growing belief in my own greatness, I learned to develop those loving eyes.

No one's life is perfect. If you accept that as true, then you must also accept that no one's life is perfectly imperfect. Every person with a great life has some flaw or challenge, which also means every person with a flawed or challenging life has some perfection.

What is your measure of perfection? What strengths do you have that you take for granted? What do you have to offer to a relationship or to an endeavor? Don't let the past hurts or the insecure version of you answer those questions. Speak to yourself in the same way you'd speak to a dear friend. Redefine yourself. Your self-perspective is directly related to your ability to change. Develop loving eyes, trust your capability, and watch it flourish.

BECOME ALLERGIC TO DOUBT AND FEAR

A Closer Look with Adam

Trusting your capability goes hand in hand with presupposing the best in yourself. It's part of the stance of belief that we advocate. You need to truly believe that you're capable of change—of living your life differently.

Think about parents who are teaching their child how to tie a shoe. Inevitably, the child will get frustrated and say, "I can't do this!" She will try to persuade them she is not a shoe tier.

The parents still have faith that, although their child isn't a shoe tier yet, she has the capability to become a shoe tier. They say things that convey a belief that she can be different:

"You can do it."

"Let me show you one more time, and then you try again."

"What is the first step?"

"Now where do you put your fingers next?"

They talk her through a change process. They don't believe her when she says, "I can't do it."

You need to view yourself and talk to yourself in a similar manner. Believe *in* yourself and not your thoughts and statements about doubt. See a better version of yourself. Maybe you're not changed yet, but you have the capability to change.

Practice this skill with other people too. Don't believe them when they say they can't do something. Believe in them and their potential. The more you work on viewing others as capable of being different, the more you'll learn to see it in yourself.

Faith is required in order to change. Elliott likes to say he's allergic to doubt and fear. Develop that same allergy. It's the best kind to have.

ELLIOTT CONNIE STREET

Diving Deep with Elliott

I lived in Boston during a lot of my growing-up years, and Boston is a walking city, so that's how I got around everywhere. I remember the day I first caught a vision of my purpose in life. It was when I was only eight or nine years old and I'd been walking around the city. When I finally got back to the street I lived on, I looked up at the street sign and thought, *One day they're going to call that Elliott Connie Street.*

No one was telling me I was great at the time. I didn't feel good about myself. This wasn't a positive era in my life. But somehow I inherently knew, if I could get through my hardships, I was going to be someone special.

I believe most people have an inherent sense of self-worth, even if it's been trampled on for a very long time. When you talk with little children, they don't just believe in themselves; they *know* they're wonderful, beautiful, and have great potential. Then life and other external factors crowd in with doubts, and they lose sight of that worth. But I would venture to say that all of us have had a glimpse of our greatness at some time when we were young, just like I did, even under harsh conditions I experienced.

Sit still for a moment and remember that time, a moment when you caught a vision of your potential. Consider how you can recapture the essence of that clarity. How would your day go, starting tomorrow, if you trusted fully in your capability? How can that get you through the most difficult times of your life? How would it make the best times even better?

DON'T SET A BAR ON YOUR CAPABILITY AND OTHERS'

A Closer Look with Adam

Randy Pausch, a computer science professor at Carnegie Mellon University, was told he had three to six months to live following a recurrence of pancreatic cancer. In 2007, one month after receiving his diagnosis, he gave a lecture at CMU called "Really Achieving Your Childhood Dreams," which became the Internet sensation known as "The Last Lecture."

When a professor at Carnegie Mellon University retires, he or she gives a last lecture, an event in a large auditorium that is recorded live. Randy was an especially beloved professor who had to retire early because of his terminal illness, and his last lecture was packed with attendees.

One of the things Randy talked about was the course he'd developed for undergraduates in which he taught them how to build virtual worlds.

There had never been a course like it before. It entailed 50 students working in randomly chosen teams of 4. Those teams were given two weeks to build a virtual reality experience. After sharing their projects, the students were then shuffled into new groups of four before starting again, building new virtual reality experiences. This process was repeated for the duration of the semester.

When the time came for the students to share their first two-week projects, the virtual reality worlds that they created blew Randy away. Their work was spectacular and went far beyond what he thought undergraduates could achieve.

It left him at a loss for how to continue to guide them. He had been a professor for 10 years at this point, and never before had he seen this level of work from his students.

Seeking advice, Randy called his mentor, Andy van Dam, who had been his professor at Brown University.

"Andy, I just gave my students a two-week assignment," Randy said, "and they came back and did stuff that, if I'd given them a whole semester [to complete], I would have given them all A's. What should I do?"

Andy thought for a minute and answered, "You go back to class tomorrow, and you look them in the eye and say, 'Guys, that was pretty good, but I know you can do better.'"

That was wonderful advice because Randy didn't know where to set the bar with his students, and he was only going to do them a disservice by setting it at all.

The act of setting a bar, whether high or low, was a limitation.

Randy followed his mentor's advice, and his students went on to excel even more. Their peers, friends, and even parents came to see them showcase their virtual worlds. Soon they had to use a big auditorium to fit all the attendees, and even then, people stood in the back and in the aisles just to squeeze in and watch.

Randy went on to teach this groundbreaking course for the next 10 years, and he never set a bar for his students.

As a solution focused therapist, Elliott has worked countless times with clients who are struggling with serious addictions or debilitating mental illnesses, and he doesn't know where to set the bar with them. Instead, like Randy, he's developed a discipline to not set a bar.

Sometimes his clients come back and say they haven't touched alcohol for a week. If Elliott had a set a bar for them, he might have just asked them to stay sober for a day. But because he didn't, they did something that exceeded his expectations.

Setting a bar is a limiting act when you don't know a person's capability. And when do you ever know someone's capability, even your own? Instead, choose to go about your transformation into your best self without placing limitations. If you set the bar low, you get in the way of your full potential. If you set the bar high, you might feel like a failure for falling short. Instead, remember you are working toward an outcome and that setting limits or exceptions isn't as powerful as noticing moments of success along your journey.

LEARNING CAPABILITY FROM HARDSHIP

A Closer Look with Adam

You may have experiences at one stage of your life that you view as problems, difficulties, or challenges, when in reality those things were preparing you for something later in life. It's helpful to learn to view those experiences differently.

As I mentioned in an earlier chapter, when I was eight years old, my mom had a heart attack and was in the hospital for two weeks, and I didn't know if she was going to live.

While my mom was in the hospital and while my dad was at work, my oldest sister, Heidi, got put in charge of doing all the laundry. She put all the whites in one of the loads and accidentally put in a red shirt too. You can guess what happened next. All my underwear turned pink. As an eight-year-old, this was absolutely mortifying. I thought, *I cannot wear pink underwear!*

Another experience I had while my mom was in the hospital was watching people bring my family food. I did not like people bringing us food—it made me uncomfortable—but at the same time, I realized that my dad couldn't make dinner for us. He was at work or visiting my mom. And I know none of my siblings or I could do it either. We were very young. That experience taught me to accept gifts and to be humble in a situation that deals with the uncertainty. In my case, was my mom ever going to come home? Learning to deal with that at eight years old helped me learn to deal with other kinds of uncertainty later in life.

That happened to me when, fast-forward many years, my wife was diagnosed with cancer. I found myself in another situation where people had to bring us food. I still hated it, but I knew that my family couldn't do it by ourselves. I knew I had to deal with uncertainty again. By watching my dad act as a single parent when I was a child, I knew I could do it now. He did it for two weeks while my mom was in the hospital, and he did it for much longer while she was recovering at home. I watched my mom hobble down the street, trying to recover, and I watched her turn around and return home, walking the other way. And I knew she could make it. I knew Becca could make it too when she hobbled around our neighborhood in between her cancer treatments. I knew it was hard, but I'd watched it happen before, so I understood the process. I understood it was necessary.

I would have never viewed my mom's heart attack as a good thing, but I learned an infinite number of lessons from it that I had to utilize again later in life. If those challenges had been happening for the first time, they would have been much more difficult. Instead, I looked at them the second time through as, "Okay, I've been through this before. I know how to do this it."

Sometimes you need to look at setbacks or challenges or hardships as "What do I need to learn now that I might need to use again later?"

Some questions that you might ask yourself when experiencing hardships or challenges might be:

- What am I learning from this experience that I couldn't have learned in any other way? What is the best way to remember this lesson so that I can draw on it next time I need it?
- What have I observed about the way I have coped with this challenge that I'm particularly pleased with? If I were to make a list of these coping skills, where would be the best place to keep this list so that I can

remember it and refer to it often, especially when things are difficult in the future?

- Even though this situation is hard, who has supported me in a way that I really appreciate? What is the best way to express appreciation to these individuals? What do I need to remember about how I accessed this support when I need to draw on it again?

ENDURING THE AFTERMATH OF HURRICANE KATRINA

Diving Deep with Elliott

Several years ago I worked with many clients who had moved to Fort Worth, Texas, from New Orleans to escape the flooding from Hurricane Katrina. This was during my internship program for graduate school, and many of my colleagues doubted Solution Focused Brief Therapy could help these people, especially when their desired outcome was wishing Hurricane Katrina had never happened.

I will never forget one of his clients, Grace (name changed), who told me a horrific story about how when she was in the flood, the raging water ripped her grandchild from her arms. She wasn't sure if she would ever see that grandchild again.

Even though Grace didn't express it directly, it was clear to me what her desired outcome was—to have her grandchild back—something beyond my ability to help her achieve. Instead of dwelling on that, I asked her, "How do you know you're strong enough to get through this challenge? How do you know you can handle whatever is coming next?"

Grace answered, "Because I've been through difficult times in my past."

"What things did you draw upon to get through those difficult times?" I asked.

We went on to have a conversation about her capability to endure difficult times.

Think of the most difficult time in your life and how you got through it. What did you learn from that experience? Can you think of another time when you applied those lessons to a new and difficult circumstance? How can you also apply the abilities and the perspectives you fostered back then to help you through your life right now?

Questions to Ask Yourself

- What helps me trust myself?
- What do I already know about myself that is worth trusting?
- What do others see in me that lets them know they can also trust me?
- Who in my life is trustworthy? How do I know that about them? What did they do to help me know that I can trust them?
- What hardships have I encountered that have really helped make me who I am today?
- What are the qualities or characteristics I have that I developed by overcoming hardships? What qualities do I have that I could only have developed because I had to work to overcome something difficult?
- What qualities do I have that I want to make sure I recognize that will help me overcome the next challenging circumstance I encounter?

PART III

The Diamond

CHAPTER 9

DISCOVERING YOUR PURPOSE

MY MOM, THE FIGHTER

Diving Deep with Elliott

My mother struggles with bipolar disorder. She has epic bouts of mania, during which she doesn't sleep for days and calls me excessively, and then she'll experience really bad dips of depression.

A few years ago, before the COVID-19 pandemic hit, my mother had been living in Texas, and she no longer needed to care for my younger brother, who was out of the nest, married, and living on his own. She called me and said, "I'm ready."

"Ready for what?" I asked.

"Ready to go home," she replied. Within about a month, she was packed up to move back to Chicago.

My family in Chicago owns two multifamily buildings that are next door to each other. One aunt owns one of the buildings and another aunt owns the other. I've got a cousin that lives there too.

It's kind of the family headquarters, where everyone congregates. When I helped my mom move back to Chicago, she moved into one of the apartments of those two buildings.

A couple of years later, Adam and I took a trip to Chicago, and I realized that my mom hadn't been having significant bouts of mania and depression. Her moods had equaled out significantly, which was astonishing since she had struggled with bipolar disorder since the '90s, when I was in high school and early college, and now she had sustained a two-year stretch without having waves of peaks and valleys that are associated with bipolar disorder.

When we visited my mom, I watched in person how different she was within the tight circle of her family, rather than in Massachusetts married to an abusive guy (my dad) or living in Texas on her own. In Chicago, my mother had reclaimed her identity. She wasn't the same woman. A healing had taken place. I wanted to understand more about how it had happened without prescription drugs or intensive treatments. All my mom had done was move back home.

My mom is one of the most caring people I know. That's her purpose. The first thing I learned about what had changed her is that she became who her siblings knew her to be. My aunts and uncles had always told me, "Your mom is a fighter."

One of my uncles, a man we called "Maine," pulled me aside on this trip and said, "It's nice to have Jenny back."

"What do you mean?" I asked.

"Your mom was always the protector of the family," he replied.

That role was hard for me to reconcile with the woman I knew, who soaking wet, was only 90 pounds. My uncle had always seemed the tougher person, a man covered in tattoos who had lived a past full of gang involvement, drugs, and prison.

"When the bullies would try to mess with us," Maine went on to explain, "your mom would go out and fight them. And now that attitude is back."

This version of my mom wasn't present while dealing with my dad during my growing-up years. But now my uncle was telling me, "It's nice to see Jenny feisty again. Her personality has returned."

Since my mom moved back to Chicago, she also became the full-time caregiver to her sister, who's much older than she is. This was a role my mom thrived in, a role that was in line with her purpose.

Simply living in her purpose was what healed my mother. It can heal you too.

A HUNTER WITHOUT A HUNTING SEASON

Diving Deep with Elliott

Over the years as I've worked with countless clients, I've witnessed again and again how, once they made changes in their life that brought them back in line with who they really are, their clinically diagnosed symptoms went away.

I once conducted therapy for a man who was in his mid-30s and had just left the military. He was suffering from PTSD and couldn't sleep through the night, and his wife was ready to leave him. All in all, he was an absolute wreck.

"I've been in the military since I was 18," he told me through tears. "I have all these skills that I can never use again, and it freaks me out. I know how to track things, and it doesn't matter in the civilian world, but it mattered a lot in the world I just left. When I think about not being able to use these skills anymore, it makes me feel like I wasted 20 years of my life, and that makes me want to kill myself."

"Where do you imagine you could apply these skills if not on the battlefield?" I asked.

"I have no idea," he replied.

"What do you mean 'I have no idea'?" I pressed, demonstrating my faith in him. "What do you think?"

Eventually he answered, "Maybe I'll try hunting."

When he came back to therapy, he was very dejected because he'd found out it wasn't hunting season. "I'm not allowed to do it," he said, frustrated with me like it was my fault. "I could be a hunter but not unless it's hunting season."

He didn't want to schedule a follow-up therapy appointment, so I wasn't sure if I'd ever see him again, but a month later he called and wanted to come back. When I met with him that time, he was glowing. He looked like a completely transformed person. He'd also brought his wife, who was waiting for him in the lobby. Things were apparently going better between them.

"What's been different?" I asked.

"I found out that, even though it's not hunting season here in Texas, people can still hunt pigs year-round," he said. "So, I went to a public hunting ground and just sat there for hours, where I could feel the wind and fresh air and be out in the grass. I started reading signs in the environment and began tracking pigs. Then a few hours later, the most amazing thing happened: I found them. I hadn't brought a weapon because I wasn't really trying to kill them. I just wanted to use my skills."

Apparently most hunters sit in a tree, put corn on the ground, and wait for a pig to come. Not very exciting. But this guy called some friends and said, "I'll tell you what. I will take you to this land, and I will spot and stalk for you," a term for ambush hunting, which he'd learned to do well in the military. His friends loved his idea. It meant they wouldn't have to sit in a tree all day. My client continued to do this every weekend, bringing up groups of people to hunt pigs.

About a year later, his wife called me and said, "He has no more signs of PTSD." She thanked me for helping him.

Why was he doing so much better? He was living according to his purpose. He was walking in alignment with who he is and using the skills he's been gifted. Doing such, he was no longer experiencing emotional dysregulation. He could just be himself.

The true cure to mental health—the true pathway to success—is walking in alignment with who you are.

GIVING PAIN A PURPOSE

Diving Deep with Elliott

There was once a time in my life when I wanted God to make me a third baseman for the New York Yankees. That's what I wanted my purpose to be. But I remember a day in college when I was 20 years old and one of my teachers pulled me aside. I swear to you, God was talking to me through her. "You should be a psychotherapist," she said.

My knee-jerk reaction was *no*! I was supposed to be on the New York Yankees. *Psychotherapist?* I'd never heard of that word before.

"A psychotherapist is a counselor," she explained. "And, Elliott, the way people respond to you is different. I've been a professor for 25 years, and the students in my classroom, they come and go. But you're special. I think you should be a psychotherapist because you'd be a very good one."

I remember thinking how that profession sounded so boring. I pictured myself sitting in an office all day, wearing a sweater vest and smoking a pipe. I didn't want to be Sigmund Freud when what I dreamed of was playing third base for the New York Yankees.

But it didn't take me long to realize that being a psychotherapist is what God had intended for me. Once I embraced that purpose, the pain from my past—the trauma I went through from dealing with a super abusive dad—went away. Why? Because when you give pain purpose, it doesn't hurt anymore. It becomes inspiration for you and others.

That's what Adam and I want to give you: inspiration so that you can walk in your purpose, experience its healing magic, and make your life the best it can be.

THE ANGEL IN THE MARBLE

A Closer Look with Adam

If people understood their purpose, their potential, and what they're capable of, it would help carry them through any challenging time. They would look forward to the future with hope and optimism. They would believe in and become the best version of themselves. If your life started falling in line with that purpose, what difference would it make to you?

Fulfillment, happiness, peace—whatever your desired outcome is—isn't contingent upon whatever is going on around you. Instead, it comes from understanding who you are—your purpose—and how you'll take the next steps in your life as that truest version of yourself.

People don't often take the time to slow down and ask themselves, "Okay, who do I want to be?" More importantly, they don't ask, "Who do I have the capacity to be? Who do I have the ability to become?" To arrive at the answer, they need to consider, "Who am I already?"

Do you know how Michelangelo's statue of David came to be? Another artist had been commissioned in 1464 to carve it from a huge slab of marble quarried in Tuscany, Italy, for the project. For unknown reasons, the artist abandoned the project after barely working on it. He'd mostly only roughed out vague legs.

Two years later, another sculptor was hired to take over the project, but he backed out very quickly because he refused to work with the poor quality of the marble.

Left with no sculptor, and too expensive to discard completely, the slab of marble sat exposed to the elements for a quarter century.

In 1501, the committee who'd commissioned the statue made a renewed effort to find another sculptor, and they settled on up-and-coming 26-year-old Michelangelo, who was given 2 years to complete the task. How he extracted the figure of David from a disproportionate and mediocre quality slab of marble was considered a miraculous process. Giorgio Vasari, an artist and writer, later described it as "the bringing back to life of one who was dead."[1]

Michelangelo took that subpar material and carved from it what now is one of the most famous sculptures of all time. Two of his famous quotes speak to me: "Every block of stone has a statue inside it, and it is the task of the sculptor to discover it" and "I saw the angel in the marble and carved until I set him free."[2]

What do you need to set free? Take the time to look deeply inward and ask yourself, "What's already inside me that isn't manifesting itself yet? What's there that I need to harness?"

Where is the stunning marble angel within you that's just waiting to be revealed?

THE DEFINITION OF PURPOSE

A Closer Look with Adam

We each have a purpose. We need to find that purpose. We need to live in that purpose. There is so much to say about purpose. I love its multiple meanings. We need to live purposefully, which means living with intention. And when we live intentionally, we live on purpose, which in turn takes us closer to the way we're supposed to be living, closer to our purpose. Like many aspects of solution focused living, this process is a self-perpetuating upward cycle.

Among the many definitions of *purpose*, some of the ones that resonate with me are "for the reason you were created" and "serving the function for which it was made" and "specific to the job needed." They all have a similar vein.

Every single one of you is here on this earth to accomplish something. You're here for a purpose, and to find fulfillment, you need to live in accordance to that purpose.

My purpose revolves around my family. They're the engine that drives me. If you were to put me in a place where I didn't have access to them, I would be miserable. If I'm traveling for work, every night I will take at least 20 minutes to FaceTime with my wife and three kids. I love my career and how I'm able to help people through it, but my job doesn't come close to how I feel for my family.

Elliott is also a huge part of my purpose. Our partnership is important, but he's also like family to me. This past December, he drove all night to make it to my house in time to celebrate my son Toby's birthday and then New Year's with us. My children call him Uncle Elliott. He's also inseparable from my purpose.

What is your purpose? What fuels you? What do you believe your role in life is?

KNOWING IF YOU'VE FOUND YOUR PURPOSE

Diving Deep with Elliott

How do you know if you've found your purpose? How do you know to trust it and follow it? If you still haven't figured out what your purpose is, perhaps learning about how Adam and I discovered our purposes will help.

My story stems from the time I almost committed suicide, which I shared with you in the first chapter of this book. My father's abuse had driven me to that point, and the thought that saved my life was that I found it unacceptable to die for his problems. I decided for the first time to start living for myself and just see what happened.

There's a movie called *Lone Survivor* that's based off true events that happened to a Navy SEAL named Marcus Luttrell. His story, on and off screen, resonates with me because of how I changed my life after being in a suicidal state for so long.

In 2005, Marcus and three SEALS were sent on a dangerous mission in the mountains of Afghanistan. Marcus was the only one of his teammates to survive a ferocious battle with the Taliban. One of those teammates was his best friend.

Among the injuries Marcus sustained were his multiple gunshot wounds, a broken back, a broken pelvis, a broken nose, and a torn shoulder—much of which happened while he endured a series of horrific falls down the mountain.[3]

Paralyzed from the waist down, Marcus didn't know what to do and was feeling sorry for himself. Then he thought of his teammates and all the training he'd been through, and he said to himself, "Get up. Let's go." He refused to lie down and die.

This part isn't shown in the movie, but Marcus began to crawl on a journey that would end up being seven miles until he received help from some Afghanistan villagers.

How did he make it those seven miles in his condition? According to a speech he later gave to a football team during his Patriot Tour,[4] he said, "I reached out and I grabbed a rock. And I reached out as far as I could, and I drew a line in the dirt in front of me. I was like, 'I'm going to crawl to that till my feet hit it. If I'm still alive, I'm going to do it again.' And that's what I did. I'd draw a line and crawl to it; my feet would hit it. I'd fall down a hill, I'd crawl up another hill, I'd draw another line. And I did that for seven miles."

In the last line of narration in the movie, Mark Wahlberg, who portrays Marcus, says, "I can never forget that no matter how much it hurts, how dark it gets or how far you fall . . . you are never out of the fight."[5]

When I learned about Marcus's story and his seven-mile crawl, I related because that's how 20-year-old Elliott handled his circumstance. After deciding to live, I didn't say to myself, "I'm going to live for me now, and I know exactly what to do." I just said, "I'm going to live *tomorrow* for me, and I'll see what happens."

Tomorrow was my line to crawl to, day by day. I was going to do things that felt right, not in a "feel good" way, but in a "necessary for survival" way. And you know what? It was hard. It required tremendous amount of courage because one of the things that felt right was calling my father and saying to him, "I've decided I want to live a life without anyone yelling at me, calling me names, or hitting me. I'm choosing a life without aggression or violence. You're welcome to join me in that life, but you have to follow those rules, which I think are pretty basic. You can't yell at me, you can't call me names, and you can't hit me."

Do you know what he replied? He said, "F*ck you."

I took a deep breath and said, "Okay, you've just broken one of the rules. Call me when you're willing to follow them."

He never called me back. We've never spoken again, and that was 24 years ago. I mourned the loss of my dad, and mourning people who are still alive is very difficult. I still hope he'll call me back one day but only if he's willing to follow my rules. On the upside, since that conversation, I now live a life where I haven't been hit, name-called, or yelled at in 24 years. And I cannot describe how good that feels.

The very next semester, I got a 4.0 in college. That was another line I crawled to, and I kept crawling to again. I kept doing things that felt right to me.

One day, all of a sudden I realized my anxiety was gone. My depression was gone too. I thought to myself, *I wonder if other people know about this—that they can change.*

If they didn't, I wanted to tell them.

I've told you about my purpose—to impact the world through love—and part of that is to remove unnecessary human suffering. This is where that purpose started. I wondered, *How many people are walking around anxious, sad, worried, and depressed and don't know that they can make choices that can completely change that?*

I once thought being anxious and depressed was inevitable, that waking up every morning and facing life was drudgery. But now I wake up every morning with excitement because I can't wait to see what the world will look like as I continue living according to my purpose.

It's because my life transformed that I wanted to help other people transform their lives. That's why I became a psychotherapist, to help people know that they don't just have to abide living a life where all the choices are made around them. They don't have to be swept away on a current without their consent or participation. They can make choices too. They can steer the boat. That requires courage, and it requires doing things differently.

How do you know if you've discovered your purpose? It's when you've found the thing that lights your soul on fire. You're making decisions that, in your core, feel right. You want to wake up in the morning.

Will you experience discomfort along the way? Yes. Will you sometimes have to crawl to a line you've drawn in the dirt and do it over and over again? Yes. But you can do hard things when there's a purpose to drive you. A purpose will give you courage to take action, discipline to stay on course, and focus to avoid distractions.

I don't wish I had a different childhood, even though I was dealt a tough hand in life. I'm sure many of you have been dealt your own. But my childhood and adolescent years built me. I grew to know that there's very little that life can throw at me that I don't have full confidence I can get through.

Now when I wake up in the mornings, I have such a different energy because I know one of two things will happen: the world will throw something at me that's going to harden me and toughen me—something I can get through—or I'll discover something amazing and beautiful in this world. That's such a contrast to how I was living before.

That's how I know problems are irrelevant. That's why I practice Solution Focused Brief Therapy and live a solution focused life. I've come to learn that people are indestructible when they're doing the thing that lights their souls on fire.

DISCOVERING YOUR PURPOSE CAN BE GRADUAL

A Closer Look with Adam

Elliott mentioned a word that stands out to me in the process of finding your purpose, and that word is *courage*. When Elliott discovered his purpose, it landed as a big, defining moment for him. But that wasn't the case for me, and it may not be for you.

Finding my purpose didn't come in an instant. It was something I had to discover over time—and something I had to discover by being courageous.

One of the things you should know about me is that I come from a great family. I have two parents who love me and who are very successful, and I'm one of five children. For the most part, we like each other and get along.

My dad and I are very similar, but we butted heads sometimes. One of the things that contributed to that is he saw something in me growing up that I didn't want to see. He would regularly tell a story about when I was a toddler and he and I played a matching game with cards. At three years old, I beat my dad in that matching game. Although I don't remember the incident, I've since heard many times how much my dad did not like that I beat him. As a child and adolescent, that translated to me as it's not okay to beat him. I shouldn't try to do so. And I shouldn't be wiser than others.

I kept living my life, got great grades, and I never did anything I wasn't supposed to do. My dad would say over and over to me, "You are the smartest child we have," which made me very uncomfortable. I did not like it. I didn't want to admit that I had knowledge, a great ability to learn things, and that learning came very easily to me. I would brush his compliments aside and reply with mean retorts like, "Then you must have very stupid children."

This was a recurring conversation between my dad and me for a long time. It wasn't until I got older and had children of my own that I started to realize how he could see things in me that I couldn't see back then.

I later realized I was going to need this intellect to graduate with a doctoral degree. I would need this intellect to teach for several years as a university professor to prepare clinicians to serve thousands of people in need. I would need this intellect to help many families directly, as a therapist, to achieve their own desired outcomes.

All these *achievements* helped me to live within my purpose of making the world a happier place and to diminish suffering. Using my intellect was necessary to live within my purpose of helping others experience and live with joy. My dad could see the possibilities of me using this intellect to achieve my purpose far sooner than I could.

When I turned 19, I decided to serve a mission for my church, which required me to be away from home for 2 years in England and then Wales. Much of what I did full time was knock on doors, trying to tell people about the beliefs I had. As you can imagine, a lot of doors slammed in my face, and it became disheartening. I had to learn to persevere with this difficult process of proselyting. I had to find that conviction in myself and focus on it more than my worry about the response I might get.

When my mission took me to Cardiff, Wales, my missionary companion and I knocked on a random man's door, who told us, "I've been waiting for you." To us as missionaries, this was like striking gold. But the man had a surprise in store, and it wasn't a positive one.

He invited us inside, and we ended up visiting with him for two hours. During every minute of that time, he berated us about how we could possibly believe in what we did. I felt like I'd gotten beaten up. And that wasn't the end of the beating. Somehow this man figured out where I lived, and a few days later, a 45-page letter arrived in the mail for me, in which the man continued to tell me I was wasting my time serving my mission.

I read the whole 45 pages, and at the end, I had to evaluate why I was doing this. I had to ask myself, "Is this in line with what I'm supposed to be doing in life?"

Elliott mentioned that his purpose involves an end to unnecessary suffering. And what I have discovered for myself is that my purpose involves helping people see their own divinity.

Even though that man in Wales disagreed with me and thought I was wasting my time, it was my job to see divinity in him. So, I reread his 45-page letter, but this time I looked for his strengths, his abilities, and his dedication. And believe me, it takes a lot of dedication to write 45 pages.

When I read the letter with that vision, it didn't bother me that he disagreed with me. It didn't bother me that he thought that I was wasting my time. It didn't bother me that he told me I was going to go to hell because I started to see him differently.

I realized if I ever expected people to shift their perspectives and live within their full potential and purpose, I'd first need to shift my perspective about them. It was a lesson I'd soon confront again.

After my mission, I was dating my soon-to-be-wife, Becca, and she introduced me to her father, who is an accountant. When we told him about our intention to get married, he asked me, as a good accountant should, "What do you want to do with your life?"

"I want to be a university professor, and I want to do counseling," I replied.

He wasn't impressed. "You realize you're going to be poor your whole life?"

"Well, I hope not," I said.

"How do you think you're going to take care of a family on that meager salary?" he countered.

This was the second time big time in my life when I chose to view someone who was being very adversarial to me in a different light. I told myself, *He's trying to take care of his daughter, and he wants to make sure that I do too.* But I also had to dig up courage and think, *I don't care if Becca's dad thinks what I'm doing is a waste of time and that it won't meet the standards of his expectations. I know this is what I'm supposed to do. By becoming a therapist and a university professor, I can help people see their own divinity.*

What that compassion and resoluteness in mind, I told him, "I'll do my very best. And that's got to be good enough."

Since this encounter, Becca's dad has been a huge supporter and advocate of the work I do. He has validated my decision and has overtly expressed to Becca that he is glad I'm part of their family. It was a nerve-wracking experience, but I have realized that once he understood that this career path was in line with my purpose, he also understood that money wasn't the only factor I was weighing in this decision. I needed to be purpose-led and be confident in my purpose or he would never have been able to get on board with my purpose.

Sometimes when people are in the process of discovering what their purpose is, others might try to persuade them that what they're doing is wrong, that they're not living the right way according to whatever set of standards. But once you find your purpose—that burning in your soul, as Elliott described—it doesn't matter what other people's opinions are. You are confident that you're doing things the right way as *you* have defined them, things that are in line with *your* purpose.

Discovering my purpose didn't occur all at once. It took time to catch on to seeing myself the way my dad saw me. It took time to see myself differently than someone who disagreed with me. It took time to see myself as someone capable to stand up to someone that I respected and say, "You might not see it yet, but I see it, and so I'm going to continue to move in the direction that's right for me, and maybe someday you'll see that it's right too."

What moments in your own life can you recall that give you a glimpse of what your purpose is? Where do you draw strength from to tell others who doubt you, "It's okay if you don't see the greatness in me. I'll keep pressing onward, and maybe someday you'll catch the vision too"?

In other words, what is the origin story of your purpose? Do you have a big defining moment like Elliott or incidents of gradual formation like me?

Even if you don't have a lot of clarity about your purpose right now, what moments can you identify that set you on the path toward finding it? What has started pushing you in a new direction?

As Elliott likes to say, you're all superheroes. And every superhero has an origin story of how they became who they are. Taking the time to recall your own origin story is important because it will help you stay committed to the rest of your journey. It helps you remember how you've become who you are, and how you'll continue to become even more heroic.

CHAPTER 10

INTRODUCING THE DIAMOND

YOUR JOURNEY TO SUCCESS

Diving Deep with Elliott

Adam and I set out on the journey we did together because we wanted to help people. That's what we still endeavor to do. We want to help you become the best version of yourself, whether you're a therapist, mathematician, scientist, or plumber. Your occupation doesn't matter. We simply want you to be the best *you*, and you can't do that without intentionality. We created the diamond model specifically with that in mind.

We invite you to embark upon the following chapters thinking about your magic, your skillset, your purpose—just wholeheartedly thinking about *you*. You may have been taught that thinking about yourself is selfish, but it's actually self-love, and you can't show love to other people without first discovering what you love about yourself.

As you go through this process, we remind you to have courage and loving eyes. We hope you gain the ability to view yourself as resourceful and hope-filled—someone who can accomplish anything. We truly believe you can. We've witnessed again and again that people are more powerful than they realize.

THE SOLUTION FOCUSED DIAMOND

A Closer Look with Adam

The diamond model is one of the biggest innovations in the field of Solution Focused Brief Therapy. It's a flowchart that includes the five skills that therapists need to master to do Solution Focused Brief Therapy effectively. It guides them through every moment of a session.

Before we created the diamond, we put in countless hours researching, studying, and reviewing recorded therapy. We analyzed how the most experienced long-term professionals were practicing SFBT. We literally traveled the world to interview these people. We even conducted a Delphi study before we came up with the diamond. This is not a random idea. This came after a decade of careful work.

Elliott was conducting a training in Chelmsford, England, when he drew this model on a whiteboard for the first time. Someone in the audience commented, "That looks like a diamond," and the name stuck. We've been calling it the diamond ever since.

Because this is a book for everyone, not just therapists, we've adapted the diamond so it works on an individual basis. Using the diamond, we'll walk you through designing in great detail the success you want to achieve.

The diamond shows five circles: desired success, history of success, resources, future success, and celebration. We've already introduced you to the top point of the diamond, desired success, but as a refresher, your desired outcome is what you're hoping for, what you want at the end of this process. You can also think of desired outcome as desired success, especially in terms of something you want to achieve or become. This success could be something you are hoping to realize, like a New Year's resolution, or it could be something bigger that might take multiple years or even a lifetime to achieve.

Moving forward, to simplify our discussion of the diamond, we'll be using the term *desired success* for both desired success and desired outcome. **Desired success** is the top of the diamond for a reason; it's the anchor point for everything else in this way of thinking.

The middle row of the diamond (from left right) contains what we call description pathways—avenues you can explore to further define your desired success.

Those description pathways are:

- **History of success:** where your desired success has shown up in the past and played a role in your life
- **Resources for success:** where you identify the strengths, qualities, characteristics, and skills you have that can help you achieve your desired success
- **Future success:** where you envision your desired success showing up in the future, usually starting with tomorrow

The final point of the diamond (the bottom circle) is **celebration**, which emphasizes praise and rewards for the changes you'll be making.

We're passionate about this process. The diamond has completely transformed the way we teach others, and the way we live our lives. We can't wait for you to reap its benefits as well!

THE PURPOSE DIAMOND

CHAPTER 11

DESIRED SUCCESS

The Top Point of the Diamond

OWNING WHAT YOU WANT

Diving Deep with Elliott

In my opinion, the most vulnerable thing you can tell another person is what you want. Whenever you expose yourself and tell people what you truly, genuinely, deeply want to achieve or become, it requires a great level of courage and an environment that is safe.

When I attended my university, I took an Intro to College class that was mandated for every freshman. I sat at the back of a room filled with about 50 students because at that time in my life, I just wanted to hide in the corner.

On the first day of class, the professor handed out a notecard to each student and asked us to write down what we wanted to be in five years.

All the students had their heads down as they intently wrote their answers . . . and I couldn't think of mine. After a few minutes of pondering, I finally wrote down something, and then everyone handed in our notecards to the teacher.

As she started looking through them, she said, "Oh, someone wants to be a dentist. Who wants to be a dentist?" A boy raised his hand, and the teacher told him all about the university program that would support that pursuit and the advisor he should talk to.

She drew another card. "Somebody here wants to be an English professor. Who is that?" A girl raised her hand, and the teacher told her about the university's English department and whom she should connect with over there.

The teacher drew a few more cards, all which continued to mention careers and graduate programs, and then she drew my card. "Somebody wrote 'alive,'" she said, looking suddenly uncomfortable. "Who was that?"

The classroom grew very quiet. I felt myself shrinking in my seat. By this point I realized I'd misunderstood the assignment. But I'd been genuine in my answer. Five years from now, the thing I most wanted to be was alive. I had just emerged from my difficult childhood, which was filled with abuse, and for the first time in my life, I was out of my house but also dealing with a tremendous amount of depression and anxiety. Anything that amounted to being aboveground and breathing I would consider a success.

"Who wrote 'alive'?" my teacher asked again. I didn't have the courage to raise my hand and own my answer. Being alive was as far as I could dream, and I didn't want to admit that. But as I mentioned in the last chapter, what got me through this difficult period was finding a purpose.

My major was marine biology, and when it was time to register for classes the next semester, I walked into my advisor's office and said, "I just want to help people."

"Then are you sure you want to be a marine biologist?" she asked.

"No," I replied. "I don't know what I want to be in this world, but I want to help people."

"Maybe you should major in psychology and become a counselor," she suggested.

"If that's a career where I can help people, then yes, that sounds good."

From that moment on, I've been obsessed with nothing more than making people feel better in life. I want every person I cross paths with, whether professionally or personally, to be a bit better for having interacted with me. I want them to smile a bit, laugh a bit, joke a bit—all in all, be uplifted. That's also what I want for you. I want this book to uplift you . . . and that's going to require you to be courageous and declare what you want.

After I found my purpose and walked in line with it, pursuing what I wanted—to help others—some pretty magnificent things happened in my life. I started seeing the light at the end of the tunnel. I started living a life with energy, and I started becoming who I really wanted to become.

It can be super scary to declare what you want because once you let others know, you become accountable to your dream. People will check in with you to see how the pursuit is going, and you're either going to have to tell them it's working or failing. But it's still very helpful to share your desired success with at least one other person because you can't get in line with your purpose until you own that that's what you're trying to do.

My difficult experiences as a child made my ability to dream dwindle. That's why at the beginning of college, my answer for where I saw myself in five years was "alive"—the most basic answer it could possibly be. But when you're living according to your purpose, you get to dream bigger.

I've been vulnerable with you in this book. I've told you my dream, the desired success I have, to make a difference in the world through love, to do my part to remove unnecessary suffering in human lives.

In sharing that, I realize how ridiculous and overly simplistic it may sound, like it's as easy as pushing a button to make such a change happen in the world. But that's truly what I want to accomplish, and I know by declaring it, some people will judge me and think I'm arrogant for even believing I can tackle this dream. But that doesn't derail me. I've worked toward my desired success for a very long time, and it continuously leads me to new goals with my solution focused organization.

To be honest, my inner fulfillment doesn't rely on those goals being accomplished. For me, it's about the journey—the lessons I learn and who I meet along the way. But you can't start that journey until you own what you're trying to achieve in the destination.

One of the people I want to impact on my journey is my mother. She went through a lot of hardship watching her children deal with what was happening with my father. She did her best to protect us and later heal us, but she often feels regret. "Did I stay with their dad too long?" she asks herself. "Did I keep them in a bad situation?" But every time I tell my mother something positive and productive about my life, I watch her regret diminish and her happiness grow. "Look at my son and what he's doing," she loves to tell other people.

That's what the journey is about for me, having those kinds of interactions in my life. Whether or not I accomplish my goals, I can still give my mother moments where she feels proud of herself in the way she raised her children. That's why solution focused living is purpose-driven, outcome-driven, and not contingent on accomplishing goals. It's about the journey. And to be on the journey, you have to claim where you're headed.

So, dream as big as you can and ask yourself, "What do I want?" If you're not afraid to declare it to another person, it's probably not deep enough. Dig deeper and find the thing you're afraid to say aloud and then say it. Write it down. Share it with someone. Claim that desire.

The payoff for your vulnerability will arrive. When you commit to what you want—when you can declare it and describe it—you'll see it come to life before your eyes. And as you embark on your journey, you'll be able to identify the milestones bringing you closer to your desired success. You'll watch it manifest into existence.

SOLIDIFY YOUR DESIRED SUCCESS

A Closer Look with Adam

The most important part of the diamond is figuring out what your desired success is. You need to take the time to solidify it. Defining and describing your desired success is the backbone of everything you're trying to become as the best version of yourself.

If you think about every successful person you can imagine—any person you admire, whether famous or in your personal life—they know who they want to be. They understand the version of themselves they have to step into to accomplish the things that they want and to be the kind of person they want to be. They know what their desired success is.

Desired success is different from a goal like a New Year's resolution or something to check off on a list of to-dos. When people think about a New Year's resolution, they typically think about something that they want to accomplish or complete. It's a behavior they want to increase, like going to the gym more often. But when we talk about your desired success, what we're getting at is you as a person. Who do you want to be? Another word that Elliott and I use in exchange for "success" is *transformation*. Who do you want to become?

Think deeper than a goal or a resolution. If you want to go to the gym more often, ask yourself, "To what end?" That question points you toward the desired success or transformation. If you *do* go to the gym more often, what will the result be? Perhaps you'll lose weight or be a healthier person—but again, to what end? What kind of person will you be if you weigh less or are healthier?

Push past just answering about behavior changes or slight changes. Instead, look at yourself and ask, "If I am the most successful version of myself, what is the totality of who I am as that version?" In other words, how would that version of you show up in other areas of your life? Perhaps the successful version of you *does* show up at the gym, or perhaps at your place of work or for your family at just the right time.

Let's say your desired success is to be strong and competent. That version of you should be able to be transported to your place of work, at home, at your place of worship, or at a park with a stranger. If you would be pleased about that version of you showing up in all those places, then you've captured a meaningful desired success. If not, think a bit longer about what version of you *would* work for all those areas.

All the prompts on the worksheet at the end of this chapter will help you define in depth "What does my success look like?" and "What does my success mean?" Tapping into that meaningfulness is so important.

Take the time to contemplate what it would mean about you as a person if you achieved your desired success. You should be pleased by the answer. It should tell you something valuable about yourself. It should help you feel like you're living within your purpose. In the same vein, your desired success should be something you feel like you need to do or to become to fulfill your sense of purpose.

With that backdrop, as you think about your desired success, what are you hoping for?

FIGURING OUT YOUR "WHY"

A Closer Look with Adam

Solution focused living is an outcome-oriented approach, not a goal-oriented one. Trying to achieve a desired outcome (a desired success) is vastly different from achieving a goal because *outcome* implies that endless possibilities exist. How to get there isn't the focus. When you *are* there is the focus. Describing the presence of your success and what difference it would make drives lasting determination and change.

If you merely focus on how to get there, you get into a rut of thinking of what you can do. For example, "What could I do to get my partner to like me better?" or "What could I do to control my tongue and not argue so much?" In contrast, when you focus on your success already being present in life, you don't have to worry about how to get there.

Let's say your desired outcome is to feel peaceful. Instead of worrying about how to feel peaceful, it's more beneficial to ask yourself, "When I feel peaceful, what do I notice that is different?" Deeply envisioning that state has more power to trigger change in your life than problem-solving about how to make it happen.

If the initial desired success you think of is a goal rather than an outcome, don't worry. Just dig a bit deeper to understand what you're hoping for.

Maybe your first answer is, "I want my partner to stop sleeping around." Now figure out why you want that. Motivational speakers bring up this topic frequently. "You've got to know your *why*," they say. In other words, if that's your goal, why is it your goal? Another way to ask this is to ask yourself, "What difference would achieving that make?"

Maybe your answer is, "My partner and I would fall in love again." Can you see how that's already a much more transformative response than, "I want my partner to stop sleeping around"? The partner not sleeping around is only part of what you want. Being in love again is a more meaningful outcome, success, and transformation.

In another scenario, let's say a father wants to lose 20 pounds. What difference would it make if he lost 20 pounds? His answer—his *why*—is that his doctor told him if he doesn't lose weight, he might not live much longer due to an increased cardiovascular risk. This concerns him because he loves his young daughter, and he wants to be around for several more years so he can attend her high school graduation.

By knowing his *why*, he can now home in on what motivates him. Statistically speaking, one of the reasons why people fail to lose weight is because they focus on the number of pounds they want to shed rather than *why* they want to shed them.

Remember, the goal is what you want on a surface level—in this case, pounds shed—but the outcome (the desired success) is what drives you to take action about it. If all you focus on is "I want to lose 20 pounds," you'll eventually lose discipline and abandon your pursuit.

You'll know once you've established a meaningful desired success when you name an internal state as your answer. What is the internal state that the father wants to achieve by losing 20 pounds so he can live long enough to attend his daughter's high school graduation? It's love. It's satisfaction in seeing all the years of his parenting finally pay off.

Solution focused living is never about the 20 pounds or the partner who should stop sleeping around or whatever you label as your problem. Instead, it's about things such as familial love and satisfaction, falling in love again, and feeling peace and acceptance. It's those internal states that matter.

HOW DESTINATIONS SET INTENTIONS

Diving Deep with Elliott

What if you feel uncertain about what your desired success is? For starters, we have a worksheet at the end of this chapter that will help you begin to articulate it. But think of the flip side of being not sure—that means you're actually a little sure. Trust in that "little sure" and write it down. You have to begin the journey to transformation somewhere.

Think of your desired success as your destination. Every time you get in your car, you have to know where you're going or you don't start driving in the first place. You have to sort that out first, and life works the same way. You have to know where you're going to start moving in a new direction.

If you don't know the exact destination, maybe you at least know the general area of where you're headed, and as you get closer, you'll find more signs and landmarks to help you figure out where you want to end up. But setting a target in the first place is so important. Once you set a target, you automatically set your intentions to achieve that arrival place.

Let's say I miss my mom and want to visit her. Once I get in the car and decide that Chicago, Illinois, is my destination, I'm setting the intention for every action between where I am currently and where I'm going. I know which left and right turns to take once I reach the city that will take me to where my mother lives.

You might be asking yourself, "But isn't it okay to just go for a drive with no destination in mind?" Of course, but in that case, you actually still do have an aim in mind. Your aim is fresh air with the windows rolled down and beautiful scenery. You're still acting in accordance with a target, a purpose, and it still sets your intentions.

One of the reasons that Adam and I don't call your desired success a goal is that your transformation isn't contingent on you arriving at your destination. Likewise, you don't have to arrive at that destination to have cause to celebrate (celebration being the bottom point of the diamond). As I mentioned earlier, fulfillment happens on the journey. You'll still become something—you'll be changed for the better—as you pursue your success.

If you don't know exactly where you want to end up, pick somewhere where you would be at least pleased to end up and start moving in that direction. You'll become something wonderful along the way that you can celebrate.

Perhaps on the journey you'll gain more clarity about what you *do* want. Maybe you even decide you don't want to be the kind of person that you were initially moving toward, but moving toward it was still useful because you needed to do that to discover your true destination.

Again, it's okay to feel unsure about what your desired success is, but it's still essential to pick a destination so you can begin becoming something you would be happy to become.

ARTICULATING AN INTANGIBLE DESIRED SUCCESS

Diving Deep with Elliott

During one of my virtual events, an attendee—we'll call him Tom—was struggling to identify his desired success. He started by saying he didn't know what he wanted. I asked if he'd be willing to let me help him figure it out, and he volunteered to do so in front of everyone so it could be a learning experience for them all. Here's the conversation we had:

Elliott: Imagine we're getting together to eat a couple of burgers a year from now on December 31. As we're enjoying our meal, I ask you, "What did you accomplish this past year that pleases you?" What would you hope you'd be able to tell me?

Tom: Hmm. I guess that I'd continued to learn and grow and be present and understand who I am in a way that makes a positive difference.

Elliott: That's wonderful! Now imagine me digging a little deeper as we eat our burgers, and I ask, "So what did you do to make sure you were learning and growing and being present and figuring out who you are?" What do you hope you would tell me?

Tom: It's going to sound counterintuitive, but I stopped trying to control it all. I just allowed things to be, which is not natural to me. I normally want to get things right and have all the answers.

Elliott: And what did you do to make sure you got comfortable not knowing and just allowing things to be?

Tom: I'm not sure yet.

Elliott: What do you hope you would do this year that would help you get used to doing this thing that you normally don't do?

Tom: I hate having to say, "I don't know," but I actually don't know.

Elliott: I understand. And how do you get comfortable in new territory, Tom?

Tom: Currently I'm just trying to be present and focusing on what I'm feeling right now rather than trying to think my way out of situations.

Elliott: How unusual is that for you?

Tom: Very unusual.

Elliott: Okay, and here we are, enjoying our delicious burgers on December 31st. How proud would you be to have gotten to that place where you became comfortable in this new way of getting to know yourself?

Tom: I would be very proud. Being able to not know how everything will turn out but still being present and actually comfortable with that—that would be a huge life change for me.

Elliott: And how would you know that was good for you? As you do this uncomfortable, hard thing, how would you know that it's beneficial to work through it and get comfortable with this new way of thinking?

Tom: As we're eating our burgers, I'd notice that I wouldn't be worried about what I was thinking, like how to be witty in our conversation. I'd just be enjoying the burgers with you.

Elliott: And if that version of you became the new you, would you be pleased by that?

Tom: I would be very pleased to actually recognize that the new me—a more grounded and self-accepting and present me—was there. Yeah, I'd be very, very pleased.

Before Tom articulated his thoughts in this conversation, he said he didn't know what he wanted his desired success to be, but as you witnessed, he actually knew more than he was giving himself credit for.

People have a tendency to think that their desired success needs to be something tangible, like a new house, a new job, or a new body without all the extra weight. But what makes life significantly better are the intangible things—states of mind, of being transformed on the inside.

And that's what Tom arrived at realizing. His desired success is to become more present, which has nothing to do with how much money he makes, what kind of job he has, or what the scale says.

Moreover, if Tom does nothing else besides focus on becoming a more present version of himself, the other things in his life will click into place. I believe that to my bones. I've seen it happen with countless clients, and I've seen it happen for me.

If I were to continue my conversation with Tom, I'd ask him questions to help his intangible desired success become more measurable. I'd start by saying, "How are you going to notice you're doing things that get you closer to becoming present in life?" It's important to find ways to notice your progress, to measure where you're at and what you're doing along the way toward your target.

That's why it's so important that Tom declares his desired success. It sets his intentions for the journey, and on the journey, he will continue to fine-tune more exactly what his desired success evolves to be. What doesn't change is Tom's purpose. His targets, his wants, his desired success—they should always stay in line with who Tom is, what his gifts are, and why he's here on this planet.

IDENTIFYING DESIRED SUCCESS THROUGH THE LENS OF DIFFERENCE

A Closer Look with Adam

In the example with Tom that Elliott just shared, notice that Tom began by saying, "I don't know what I want." And through Elliott's questions, Tom answered, in essence, "Well, I know that I want something different. I've been living life this way for a long while now, and I want things to change."

If you're in a similar situation as Tom and having a hard time nailing down your desired success, think about the lens of difference that we talked about in the stance chapters, and ask yourself these difference-oriented questions:

- If something was different, what would you like to be different?
- And if *that* was different, who would notice?

- What would they notice?
- What would you do differently?
- How would doing something differently make a difference to you?
- Phrased a little differently, some of these questions might look like:
- What difference am I looking for in life?
- If I followed through and achieved that difference, what difference would that make to me?

Your answers to those questions will get you much closer to a meaningful desired success. If you can identify the differences you want and what difference it makes, those are things you can move toward to feel successful. They're things that set you on the path to becoming the best version of yourself.

Another way that can help you clarify your desired success is to involve people you trust with the process. Who can you talk to about your intentions and targets? Who can ride alongside you on your journey? Who can check in on you to see how it's going? Who will notice when you're moving toward that place of success?

Even just thinking about what those people would do or notice differently is a helpful exercise. Envisioning their actions and responses, as Elliott guided Tom to do at their imaginary dinner together, is a way of manifesting what you want to have happen and describing it in further detail.

A difference-oriented lens is a meaning-oriented lens. Thinking about difference is a way to gauge how meaningful your desired success is. From there, you can tweak it to make it more impactful.

COMPLETING THE DESIRED SUCCESS WORKSHEET

A Closer Look with Adam

At the end of this chapter is a worksheet to help you home in on your desired success. Try to be as specific as possible when you answer each question, and don't be worried if your desired success starts to change in the process. These questions and your answers are meant to guide you in the process of articulating what you want in more detail. Your desired success should become clearer as you proceed. We're at the very beginning of your journey, and this is just the first step. What you want will come into greater focus as you keep moving forward.

You'll notice that one question appears on the worksheet again and again: "What else?" Be sure to answer that question every time, and feel free to add more "What else?" questions as you see fit. Answering "What else?" as many times as possible will help you delve much deeper and pinpoint your desired success and the meaning it holds for you.

The page after the worksheet has been left blank on purpose. You can use it for more space in answering your questions, or if you're a visual person, you can depict your responses in a way that's more creative, such as a drawing or diagram.

Lastly, be warned that answering these questions might feel hard, but we encourage you to see that as a good sign. Compare it to the pain of sore muscles at the beginning of a fitness journey. Those muscles have to break down to build up stronger. Your mental muscles need to do the same. Keep pushing through when you don't know the answers right away. It's an indication that you're building something worthwhile, and that something takes effort.

Once you're finished with the worksheet, take a moment to reflect on your answers. How was it to think that much in depth about your desired success? What surprised you the most about what you wrote down? How did this exercise let you know how important your desired success is?

What is your desired success?

Who would be impacted by you achieving this success?

What would it say about you if you could achieve this success?

What else?

What else?

What difference would achieving this success make in your life?

What else?

What else?

CHAPTER 12

HISTORY OF SUCCESS

A Diamond Description Pathway

THE JOURNEY IS THE REWARD

Diving Deep with Elliott

I've been traveling to LA a lot more these days and meeting people who are in the entertainment world. One of these is Tony Rock, a successful actor who's been on lots of TV shows and tours as a comedian.

I went to one of his comedy shows and got invited backstage. Tony had heard of the solution focused work I'm doing, and we ended up talking for about an hour. During that time, Tony asked me an important question: "When you teach people about persistence and sticking to their plan for success, how do they know they're sticking to something that works for them? Like, how do you talk to people about the pain of persistence versus abandoning the effort?"

"Well, you need to persist when it's in line with your purpose," I answered. "And you have to be able to detach the rewards from the purpose." In other words, don't do something to achieve specific rewards because being on the journey of purpose is the reward itself. "Tony, I guarantee you that on your pathway to being a famous comedian, there was a moment where you knew this was what you were supposed to be doing."

He got kind of emotional and replied, "Yeah, that's totally true." He told me about that moment, the origin of his dream and what we call in the diamond the "history of success."

To set this story up, you need to know that comedians get paid next to nothing—I'm talking as little as $20 or $30 per show—until the time in their careers that, if they get lucky, they finally break into the business in a huge way.

"One day I was performing in New York City," Tony said, "and when the comedy show ended, the owner of the club told me, 'Not enough people came tonight for me to pay you.' So he gave me chicken wings instead."

As Tony rode the subway home that night, eating his chicken wings, he thought, *Regardless of how much I ever get paid, I could do this for the rest of my life.* "It was in that moment," he said to me, "that I decided to be a comedian, regardless of the rewards. Being a comedian was the reward itself."

I've thought about that a lot, and I believe it's totally true. In my case, being a psychotherapist and a helper is the reward itself.

For Tony Rock, money wasn't his focus. He got paid in chicken wings when he decided he could be a comedian for the rest of his life. That didn't happen during his first million-dollar TV deal. It didn't happen during his first sold-out arena. It was when he was eating chicken wings on a subway in New York that he realized he just loves what he does.

That's what I want you guys to fall in love with as well—the journey. When you do, the rewards will take care of themselves. They'll show up naturally and when they're meant to.

To help you fall in love with the journey, ask yourself these questions about your desired success: "How do I know I'm on a pathway that's good for me? What has already happened in the history of my life to confirm this?"

You need to know the answers because whatever path you've chosen will be challenging. Ascension to success is more difficult than just focusing harder on what you want. In reality, your ability to overcome any difficult moments on your journey is directly connected to how much you believe in what you're doing and how much you know you're on the right path.

As you remember the origins of that path—that dream—you'll gain the strength you need to persevere and overcome any obstacles.

YOU CAN'T CRAVE SOMETHING YOU HAVEN'T SAMPLED

Diving Deep with Elliott

When speaking about the history of success, people often ask me, "What if I haven't had a past experience of my desired success?" There is no such thing. If people say they want something, it means they've at least had a sample of it at some point in the past. People cannot crave or yearn for something that they haven't touched.

To help this idea hit home, let me tell you about my first visit to New Zealand. After day one of teaching at a conference in Christchurch, the wonderful woman who was hosting me asked what I would like for dinner. She knew that when I travel, I like to try foods that I can't get easily back home in Texas, so she introduced me to a popular New Zealand food that I'd never heard of before called *kebabs*.

Kebabs are different from what we refer to as kabobs in the United States, which are more like a skewer with meat and vegetables. Instead, this kebab was like a big wrap filled with sauce and meat and yogurt and whatever else I requested to put inside. When I took a bite, it was utterly delicious and glorious.

If Adam were to say to me, "Elliott, what do you want to eat today?" I now have a file folder in my head for "kebab." I can answer,

"I would like to find a kebab shop." I couldn't have done that before because I had no file folder for it, no access point. Anytime you realize you want something, that's your evidence that you've had it before.

Continuing to use the food analogy, even if you haven't eaten something in the past, you had to at least have been exposed to it to want it currently. Maybe you've seen other people eat it or heard people talk about it or had at least a bite of it. You've had some kind of experience with it. Otherwise, you wouldn't know that you want it. Again, in some sense, you can't crave something you haven't tasted before.

Once you own that history, you can then reflect on how you noticed that instance of your desired success, why it was important to you, and how you realized you wanted more of it.

Presuppose the best in yourself and trust that you have at least sampled your desired success to want to crave it again.

IDENTIFY YOUR ACCOUNTABILITY OF SUCCESS

A Closer Look with Adam

One of the presuppositions we maintain in solution focused thought is believing that people *had* to contribute something to bring about the past instances of their desired success. They want more of what they've sampled before, and what happened before didn't just come about by chance.

People will insist that they didn't have a hand in it coming about or that they don't remember any specifics, but if you give yourself time to think about those instances, and you do so in a positive headspace, the answers will come. People tell us time and again, "I remembered things I didn't know that I remembered."

Through research, we know that positive emotion and its impact expands a person's vision—not just current or creative vision but also memory vision. People start to remember more than they knew they remembered.

People often take for granted the moments that their desired success is present. They say things like, "Ninety-nine percent of the time I deal with this problem, and I want that to be less." They minimize that one percent of the time. "I guess I'm happy sometimes," they relent, "but not very often."

Remember that solution focused thought is difference-led, so be sure to highlight difference through the questions you ask yourself, such as, "What is it about that one percent of the time that's different for me?"

Sometimes people claim that they've never been happy, they've never gotten along with their partner, or they've never been confident, but again remember that if you say you want something, it means you must have at least sampled it at some point in your life.

Be patient and persistent as you try to articulate the origin of your dream and your instances of success because doing so takes a lot of effort. Remember to focus on how you contributed. What happened that made your desired success show up?

Once you take the time to examine those instances and identify what made you accountable for them, you can easily pivot to the present and ask what you can replicate from back then to help bring about your desired success more consistently now. Envision how you would notice that happening and how it would make a difference in your life.

People take their greatness for granted. They often have a long history of "problems," so they overlook their history of success. As a result, they might not catch those instances of success when they happen again.

But "problems" always have exceptions, and instances of desired success always exist. Think about it in this context: If you had a headache your entire life from the moment you were born until today, how would you know you had a headache? There must have a moment when the headache disappeared or reduced in intensity that let you know it was solvable and therefore a "problem." If it never disappeared or reduced in intensity, you wouldn't know you had a problem.

Count on the fact that there will be an exception whenever you first think *never. Always* and *never* are words that should immediately tip you off to remember the rule of exceptions and from there be able to examine in depth your history of success.

We want you to notice those instances of success. Reflecting on them in the past in detail will help you recognize them when they come back. Each time you recognize an instance, you'll get a boost of confidence to help you continue forward on your journey.

Description pathways on the solution focused diamond have the same impact whether they're about tomorrow (your future success) or looking backward (your history of success) because it's the details of the success that are transformative, not the timeline of those details.

THE IMPORTANCE OF YOUR HISTORY

Diving Deep with Elliott

The most important lesson I've learned as a professional practicing and teaching Solution Focused Brief Therapy is how important your history is. Your history is where you've demonstrated that you are truly a champion capable of accomplishing anything and doing so with unbelievable resources and potential.

Where you come from matters, even if it's from a difficult place because the fact that you got out of it is the evidence that you are capable of your wildest dreams.

When I entered this field, I remember telling some of my colleagues that I wanted to open a private practice. They told me it would be impossible, but I still did so in the fall of 2008. That was in the midst of the economy crashing, but I had no fear. Why? I'd survived my childhood without an addiction, without the desire to abuse women, without all the statistics that laid out who I was supposed to become. That trained my brain to not fear failure.

Train your brain to not leave your past behind. Reflect on your history and collect all the bits of goodness from it so you can carry them into the future. Whatever it is you're in pursuit of, your history of thinking about that and knowing it's possible is incredibly valuable. The first step to accomplishing anything is believing it's possible. As you dig into your past, you'll be surprised to find evidence for the future that your dreams are possible. I promise they are.

FACING CANCER BY DRAWING UPON THE HISTORY OF SUCCESS

A Closer Look with Adam

In solution focused thought, we highlight strength, ability, and capability. We hold the stance of believing in people and seeing them as powerful. When people establish that they want a desired success, they sometimes falter, realizing it will take hard work. But when you presuppose the best in yourself and trust your capability, you'll remember you've done hard things before, you've managed difficulty, and you've overcome challenges.

Your history of success doesn't have to be a direct copy of the instance you're wanting now. But it can still translate and be relevant. If you want to be happy in your work environment, you don't have to recall being happy in your job before to draw lessons from it. You can instead think of when you were most happy in your life.

Perhaps that happened when you were a five-year-old kid and didn't have a job. You can still reflect on and describe that happy kid and envision those qualities you had returning to your present life. If the essence of those qualities showed up at your work environment, how would you notice them? What difference would it make?

As I mentioned in an earlier chapter, in May 2019 my wife was diagnosed with breast cancer. I found out when I was out-of-state with Elliott—we were teaching at an event in Florida. After my wife had a routine doctor's appointment, she called and said, "They're doing more tests, and I'm not quite sure what it means."

"Do you need me to come home?" I asked, concerned.

"No, I think I'll be okay," she said. "I'll call you when I get the results."

Nervous, I went back to where I was teaching. "At some point, I'm going to get a phone call," I told Elliott, "and I'll need to step out."

Soon enough, my phone rang in my pocket, and I left the room again.

When I answered the phone, my wife was crying. I knew whatever test results she had received weren't good.

"What's going on?" I asked.

"I got diagnosed with breast cancer," she said.

My mind started to race. How could this be happening? What would happen to *her*? As I stood there for a minute, taking in the news, the only thing I could come up with to say was, "How do you know that, no matter what happens, you're going to be okay?" And by *going to be okay*, I didn't even mean that she was going to live. I just meant that she would be okay as she went through the process of battling cancer.

My wife cried for a bit more and then paused to compose herself before she said the most profound thing I believe anyone could say in that moment. "Because I've done hard things before."

We spent about a half an hour talking about the hard things that she in particular had been through and how we had been okay through those times. Her history of success wasn't literal to her present circumstance. She had never battled cancer before to know how to battle it now. But she *could* draw from other hard things she'd endured and overcome.

After that phone call, I went back into the room where I had been teaching with Elliott. He looked at me anxiously and gave me a thumbs-up, but I had to give him a thumbs-down. His shoulders fell. He knew the outcome wasn't what we were hoping for.

The time came for my wife to undergo surgery to have the cancer removed. Afterward, she and I drove our kids from Georgia to Virginia, where my sister lives. My sister had offered to watch our kids for a while so my wife and I could spend some together and focus on her starting chemotherapy.

After we dropped off our kids, we embarked on our drive back to Georgia. During those nine hours, we revisited the idea of "You've done hard things before."

I said, "Knowing tomorrow that you have to do your first round of chemotherapy, and not knowing what that's going to be like, what do you know about yourself that lets you know you can do this hard thing? What have you learned about yourself, as you have dealt with other hard things, that you are glad you know going into this hard thing? What will tell you that you are using that knowledge and those qualities about yourself this time?"

We went back in time and talked about the hard things we had done before in the context of how we overcame them.

What skills did we use to make it through? Who were the helpful people around us who contributed to helping us accomplish and endure those hard things? In essence, we were doing a blend of history of success and resources—both description pathways on the solution focused diamond.

We talked about the two times my wife had experienced miscarriages and how one of those miscarriages happened on Mother's Day. We talked about the women who had reached out to her, women who had also experienced miscarriages. They rallied around her and supported her and shared how they had recovered. Family members also came to spend time with us and helped us keep going.

My wife and I also talked about how, at that point in our lives, we had moved across the country four times during our marriage. We talked about how hard it was to leave our families and friends and support systems and how in each move, we were going to a place we had never been to before.

Again, we talked about those hard times in the context of how we endured and overcame them. We remembered how our church community supported us and how financial help was also given.

Over this nine-hour conversation, we realized that, although those times in the past were difficult, in the end they didn't drag us down. They weren't too hard to overcome. Instead, they were experiences that made us stronger, events that held us together, ways we learned about ourselves, times we discovered who we were. We realized we could take all that strength with us as we faced this new challenge in our lives. We could bring all the people, the networks, the experiences, and the memories.

That conversation was like an anchor to us throughout the nine months of treatments that Becca endured. On the particularly hard days, we would reflect on what we were learning this time that we wanted to make sure we didn't forget. On the particularly good days, we made sure to be extra grateful for the smallest moments of relief. On days where support came from individuals bringing us dinner, sending flowers and cards, or calling with messages of support, we made sure to take note that our support system was rallying around us again.

Because we had taken time to think about our history of managing hard things, we were so much more aware of when history repeated itself in the best ways possible. That's the real power of having a history-of-success conversation.

DRAWING POWER FROM THE PAST

Diving Deep with Elliott

Understanding your journey is incredibly important, and I want to tell you why. Your brain does a funny thing when you look backward and assess how far you've come. I remember one day I spent in London with my aunt. We walked to the London Zoo, walked through the zoo, and then started walking back to our hotel. It felt like we'd been walking a bazillion miles by the point.

The walk back to our hotel was down a very long and straight line of a street, and as we passed Buckingham Palace, I was done. Cooked. My feet were hurting. It was beginning to rain. I didn't think I could take another step. As I hunched over, exceptionally tired, I just so happened to look behind me, where I saw miles and miles up the street we'd just walked down. Amazed at how far we'd gone without realizing it, I felt myself gain the energy I needed to continue forward.

The origin story of your desired success has that same power to rejuvenate you because at some point as you pursue your success, it's going to become so difficult that the only way you're going to be able to sustain your momentum is to measure where you've come from—your origin, your history—to where you are on this day.

Life can be very difficult, so it's helpful to be reminded of the strengths you've accumulated so far and why your dream was so important to you in the first place. I've never forgotten who I was at 16 or 19, the struggles I had, and where I started from. Reflecting on the past gives me such a tremendous source of energy because I can measure who I am today versus where I began. Most importantly, when I think about my history, I make sure to do so in an uplifting way.

The questions you ask yourself matter. I tend not to ask things like, "How did I let this happen?" and "What mistakes did I make?" Instead, I ask questions that build me up and produce kind answers. I practice the discipline of only talking to myself with belief because the messages you give yourself are impactful.

I want you to have the perspective of those same loving eyes as you spend some time in your own origin story. Sort it out for yourself and draw power from it.

As you describe your history of success, you'll begin to act consistently with your desired success—what you want now. You'll begin to live it more purposefully.

HISTORY CAN BE RECENT OR FROM LONG AGO

A Closer Look with Adam

As you examine your history of success, you may recall as far back as your young childhood or as recent as the last couple of months. Your history can even start with a conviction you had a few minutes ago. Keep your mind open to a wide range of time frames when it comes to your past.

Furthermore, your history of success doesn't have to begin with the target of knowing where you're going and what your desired success is. You may not have formed that concrete idea in the past.

You may not even realize that any evidence of it ever existed before now. But memory is fascinating and can reveal more than you may first give it credit for.

One of the misconceptions about memory is that it's static or an accurate depiction of what happened. But there's a lot of research to show that people's memories are influenced by their current situations. They recall things and filter them through their current understanding and current experience.

If you limit your history of success to only the last two or three months, you might accidentally discredit meaning-making opportunities about memories that go further back in time. Your recent history isn't to be taken for granted, but if you push yourself, you'll find evidence from long ago that maybe you were overlooking or misinterpreting—little instances that showed you were moving in the right direction. You'll find them when you're in the mindset of looking for and noticing evidence that the transformation you're hoping to achieve is possible.

When you do, you'll tap into characteristics you've had for however many years that are relevant to what you're going through now, as well as important people and relationships from the past that prove you can move in the direction you're trying to move in now. Bits and pieces of your history will come back into play, and you'll ascribe new meaning to them in your current situation.

The longer you allow yourself to dig into your past, the more you'll find additional and relevant history from which you can draw new strength and purpose.

THE PROMISE I MADE TO MY GRANDMA

Diving Deep with Elliott

Origin stories are so important, especially origins of a legacy. I'll tell you about one of mine and how it changed my life.

During my adolescent years, I moved with my mom and younger brother to Texas. My older brother had already moved away for college, and the rest of us wanted to get my mom as far away from my dad as possible and closer to my aunt, her sister.

During this time, my mom started to show signs of some mental health challenges, which were appropriate for having gone through what she did. Meanwhile, our family was trying to get used to a world with no violence in it, which is ironically when things got harder. Everything was new and different and challenging.

While we were all staying at my aunt's house, my grandmother came to visit, and she is the matriarch of the family, the most powerful woman you could possibly know. One day we were all sitting at the kitchen table, having a meal, and when we finished, everybody got up to leave, including me. But my grandmother said, "Elliott, can you stay here for a second?"

"Sure," I replied, and when I turned and looked at her, she had tears rolling down her face. This was the first time in my life that I'd ever seen her crying.

"I need you to make me a promise," she said.

"Sure, Grandma. Anything," I answered, still shocked by her emotions.

"Promise me you will take care of your mother."

I nodded. "I promise I'll take care of my mother."

She grabbed me by the collar of my shirt and said again, "Promise me."

"Yeah, Grandma." I swallowed and said one more time, "I promise."

She gave me a hug unlike any hug I've had, before or since.

I didn't realize it at the time, but my life changed in that moment. Even to this day, I run almost everything I do through the filter of keeping that promise to my grandmother. It's a way of checking that I'm still living according to my purpose.

My grandmother passed away in 2015, but I still feel like she's with me and a part of my life because that moment shifted how I live and do things and respond to my mom. I carry the legacy that my grandma handed off to me.

A couple of years ago, my mom texted about some bill she'd received that was double the amount she'd expected. "Can you send me some money?" she asked, which I'd been encouraging her to do if she ever got in a bind. I'm not rich, but compared to how we grew up, I'm super rich, and I want my mom to know that she doesn't have to worry about finances anymore, something she's spent her life doing.

"Sure, Mom. No problem. Anytime you need anything, let me know," I wrote, putting a smiley face emoji at the end of my text.

She wrote back, joking, "I could get used to this smiley face."

I grinned and thought, *I wish I could show this text message to my grandmother* because this is the life my grandmother was trying to help my mother have, a life without stress and worry because she had been through so much.

Of all the things I've done—I've traveled around the world and written books and given keynotes—by far the thing I'm most proud of is the way I've kept that promise to my grandmother.

There's a power to knowing the origin of your mission—your dream, your desired success—especially when it involves a legacy story. There's strength that comes from understanding the fuel that powers your engine. But most people don't take the time to think about it or talk about it, so they miss out on a wonderful opportunity to fill up their tanks, rejuvenate themselves, and recommit to their purpose.

Take a moment to talk or write about the origin behind why you want to be the person you want to be. Consider if it involved another person, like it did with me and my grandmother. Reflect on the moment you got on that path, the moment that pointed you in a certain direction. Sit in that space and let your history remind you of your passion and where it came from so it can give you continued strength to persevere in your desires.

THE LEGACY YOU CARRY WITH YOU

A Closer Look with Adam

Every human being on this planet has a hero in the history of their own life's story. Exploring your yesterdays is so important because that's where your hero is.

In 2021, Elliott and I spent two weeks on a trip visiting prominent places associated with the civil rights movement, where we interviewed several people. We learned that an entire generation of civil rights leaders, including Medgar Evers and Martin Luther King Jr., were inspired—and we use that word sensitively—by the death of Emmett Till.

Everybody has been inspired by someone, and by asking them to consider who impacted them most, and why, you can learn what and who truly inspired them. One of our favorite ways to do that is to ask what we call "legacy questions."

A legacy is when you were at your peak, when your desired success was present, what actions you took to make it present, and the qualities and characteristics you drew upon to make that possible.

In the context of the diamond and its description pathways, reflecting on a legacy happens at the intersection of history of success and resources. On the one hand, you're thinking about who taught you a resource, but you're considering how that legacy was handed off to you in the past.

Here are some examples of legacy questions you can ask yourself:

- Where did you learn to be brave?
- Where did you learn that you were the kind of person that was capable of being happy?
- Who helped you realize that you had what it took to be confident?
- What was that like?
- How did that process happen?

- How did you know you were receiving it?
- What did it mean to you when that person handed this legacy off to you?
- How did you let them know you were pleased that you had inherited this legacy?

As you reflect on where your legacy came from, you'll often remember the most important people in your life—people who changed you for the better.

After you think about your legacy and whom it's associated with, you can then ask yourself, "And if somehow that person could see me now, what would they notice to let me know I'm carrying that legacy on in just the right way?" or "What do they see in me that lets them know I'm holding their legacy with honor?"

There's so much power that can come through reflecting on the past. Don't focus so hard on the future that you forget the strength of your history. Its lessons—lessons you've learned firsthand—are invaluable in the present and beyond.

MIXING LEGACY WITH RESOURCES

A Closer Look with Adam

Before you transition into thinking about a legacy in your life, it's often helpful to first identify an important resource. Consider answering the following questions to get there:

- What is a characteristic or skill you have that you are most proud of?
- If the answer is a skill, what characteristic do you have inside you that lets you know you're good at it? (Between this bullet point and the one above, you should arrive at a characteristic, which is a personality quality they have that influences their behavior.)

- Who taught you that this characteristic is something you should value?
- How did you learn from that person that this characteristic is something you should value?
- How did that person communicate that to you?
- How did you let that person know you were pleased by learning it from them?
- What difference do you think your response made to that person?
- What difference does it make to you to realize you were connecting to that person in that manner?
- If you could make that person proud in a way that is true to the values they instilled in you, what would be the best course of action to do that?
- What does it mean to you that you can carry that person's legacy forward in your life?

That's the essence of examining a legacy that's focused on a resource, such as a characteristic in the example above. The questions center on the difference it makes to have received a resource as a legacy from someone important in your life.

The powerful thing about describing your history of success (in this case, doing that through a legacy) is that, even though you're reflecting on something that's happened in your past, you're now more likely to think about how it applies to your present and future circumstances. In other words, the past impacts what you do now, and it causes you to transform.

DIGGING DEEPER INTO THE HISTORY OF YOUR SUCCESS

A Closer Look with Adam

When did you first discover the origin of your desired success? How has that impacted you from that time until this moment, where you're going to start moving in an intentional way toward that success?

When you think back to the origin of your desired success, how did you know that you'd be living within your purpose if you pursued it? If it was a gut sensation, how would you further describe that gut sensation? What did it feel like? What did it mean to you? How did you know that feeling was a good thing?

Now, link that back to what you wrote down as your desired success in the previous chapter. Did you get that same gut sensation again, the one that tells you "This is right?" If not, how does your mind or body let you know that you experienced something to confirm your desired success is in line with your purpose and what you should be pursuing?

Let's say you arrive at the word *wholeness*. Continue to pull apart that word. How would you recognize wholeness as you move forward toward your desired success? If you make decisions that are consistent with wholeness being present, how would other people recognize that wholeness in you?

As words like *wholeness* come to you that help further delineate what your desired success is, make sure you write them down. The more complete you can make your desired success, the more likely you are to recognize it as you move toward it, which will keep you on the path to succeed.

WORKSHEET INSTRUCTIONS

As you answer this next set of questions, remember that the history of success is a description pathway of your desired success. Your history includes manifestations of you living in your purpose and working toward what you want, even if that means back when you just started to dream about it.

That dream is attainable, even if you can't see it right now. When what you want is in line with your purpose, you're unlocking your magic—unlocking what makes you uniquely you.

In the first question, we want you to think about the origin of your dream. In other words, when did you start to imagine a new and different future for yourself, one where your desired success was present? Even if that's something you're just beginning to unlock, start to think about what has led you to this point. The more detailed and specific you can get about your dreams, the more meaningful and impactful they become.

Don't be dissuaded if thinking about your past is difficult. It might be a muscle you haven't stretched before or one you haven't used in a while. It might also be hard to find times when you feel you experienced moments of success in the past. But remember it can be as small as a taste you're now craving again.

What details tipped you off that your desired success is something you wanted? How did you know that the taste you were sampling was something you wanted to have in full measure?

It's also helpful to consider what you want to hold on to from the past. What do you wish to keep the same? What are you proud of? What lessons have you learned that you want to carry forward?

When you're finished completing the worksheet, reflect on what stood out to you. What did you learn about the history that's already happening as far as your success?

The past is a treasure trove of meaning-filled moments that showcase your strengths, relationships, sparks of dreams, instances of success, and more. By taking the time to realize how far you've come, you'll gain confidence in how far you can still rise, overcome, and achieve.

Think about the origin of your dream. When in your life did you know this was what you wanted to achieve?

____

____

____

____

____

____

What was going on in your life at the time you decided this success was important?

____

____

____

____

____

____

____

Why is it important for you to achieve this dream/success?

What steps have you already taken to help you achieve this dream?

CHAPTER 13

RESOURCES

A Diamond Description Pathway

THE #1 DRUG DEALER IN WACO, TEXAS

Diving Deep with Elliott

My first job in this field was at a halfway house for teens who had been incarcerated in juvenile corrections facilities in Texas—basically prison for youth. This halfway house was a transitional living facility for teens who had turned 18 and were released from prison because they had aged out of the system. The then-named Texas Youth Commission (now known as the Texas Juvenile Justice Department) required them to spend time at a halfway house before they were sent home.

The halfway house I worked at was a collection of apartments in a terrible location, right across the street from the biggest drug houses in Dallas. That couldn't have been easy for one of the kids I worked with named Little Waco.

I met him at a time in my career when I was becoming significantly better at Solution Focused Brief Therapy. I'd made strides largely because I learned how to be impressed by my clients, even people like Little Waco.

Little Waco was tall and Black and had *Waco* carved into the side of his hair. He was 18, but he had gone to prison at age 14 for being the biggest drug dealer in Waco, Texas. That fact was obviously concerning, but on the other hand, it was pretty impressive, and because I focused on being impressed by him, it changed the way I asked him questions.

One day during a group therapy session at the halfway house, I said to Little Waco, "Obviously dealing drugs wasn't good—look at all the trouble it caused you—but I am curious, how did you become the biggest drug dealer in Waco, Texas?"

"Can I get up and show you?" he asked. With my permission, he walked up to a whiteboard at the front of the room. "Rule one," he said as he wrote it down, "never get high off your own supply."

Now I've been a lot of things in my life, but thankfully I've never been a successful drug dealer or user, so I asked, "Why not?"

"Well, there are two reasons," he explained. "If you use drugs that you buy wholesale, then you'll be cutting into your own profit." Keep in mind this is an 18-year-old kid saying this, a kid who established these rules when he was 14. "Also, drugs alter your way of thinking, and you have to be sharp when you're running a big enterprise because you'll be a target." I nodded to show that I was following.

"Rule two," Little Waco said, writing it on the board with his dry-erase marker. "Diversify."

"What do you mean?" I asked.

"Don't just sell one drug. You've got to sell multiple drugs." He explained that the drug he first introduced to his gang was meth, but he later expanded with marijuana and various pills.

"Rule three," he continued, "build a staff."

"Build a staff?" I repeated, implying that I needed clarification.

"Yes. If you're going to sell drugs, you've got to take over street corners. I'm only one person, so I can only be on one street corner.

But if I have lots of people working for me, we can strategically spread out to other street corners. Another benefit of having a staff is that they'll get caught with the drugs instead of you. If they do get caught, you have to immediately call them and say, 'If you don't snitch, I'll save a bunch of money to give you for when you get out of jail or prison.'" Unfortunately for Little Waco, this was the reason he was sent to prison—one of his staff snitched.

He had a few more rules and wrote them all down for the group in the room. I looked at this list and this kid, and I was honestly amazed. Someone with a seventh-grade education was telling me how to buy something wholesale and how to profit first.

Yes, Little Waco had made bad decisions, but he was also incredible, and I was concerned for him. He knew drug dealing this well, and in a couple of weeks the halfway house would be sending him home, where he would likely go back to selling drugs.

How could I help Little Waco? Well, it just so happened that he was full of resources.

I walked up to the whiteboard and erased "Rules of Dealing Drugs," which he had written at the top of his list. I turned to him and asked, "What if I challenge you and said that I want you to sell something that doesn't have the potential to send you to prison? What would you call this list instead, and how would you change it?"

"Hmm," he said, mulling over my questions as he looked back and forth from me to the board. "I think it's the same list."

"Give me an example," I said.

He uncapped his marker and wrote at the top of the list "Rules of Selling CDs." This was in the early 2000s, when CDs were popular.

"Can you tell me how this list is the same?" I asked.

"Well, I still can't use my own supply."

"Why not?"

"Because if I buy CDs wholesale and I open the shrink-wrap to play them, then I can't sell them anymore, so I'd be cutting into my profit."

I nodded. "What else?"

"I'd still have to build a lot of staff."

"How come?"

"I'd want my CDs in multiple malls in order to sell a lot of them, so I'd need a bunch of employees." He went on to describe in detail how he could sell CDs with the same list of rules that he'd used to sell drugs.

A couple of weeks later, Little Waco approached me in the halfway house and gave me a big hug. "Hey, Mr. Elliott," he said. "I'm being released and going back to Waco. And I hope I never see you again." I smiled because that was a good hope. No one wants to return to a halfway house.

Several years later, I found myself at a car dealership getting my oil changed. I knew I was going to have to wait for a while, and I don't sit still very well, so I went for a walk around the dealership. When I was in the used car part of the lot, a tall Black man started walking toward me.

Panic zinged through my body. I realized I was blood in the water for any salesperson, and I didn't intend to buy a car today.

The man came within 10 feet of me and paused. "Mr. Elliott?"

I shifted on my feet, disoriented. The only people who ever called me Mr. Elliott were the kids I'd worked with at the halfway house many years ago. "Yes?"

"It's me, Little Waco."

I blinked twice. He no longer had *Waco* carved into the side of his hair, and he was wearing a tie and a crisply ironed shirt, but I finally recognized him as the boy I knew when he was 18.

He started crying and rushed over, throwing his arms around me.

"Hey, man," I said, patting him on the back. "How are you doing?"

He pulled away and brushed the tears from his eyes. "I've been wanting to find you for years. After I got home from the halfway house, I realized I didn't have to sell drugs anymore. I realized I'm not good at selling drugs; I'm good at selling. When I saw a job listing for a car salesperson, I thought, *I can do that.* I'm now the head of sales here for the used car department."

Now that would have been impressive at any car dealership, but it was especially impressive at this huge car dealership.

"I have to thank you for this job," he said, weeping and hugging me again. "But that's not the biggest thing I want to thank you for."

"Oh?" I asked, curious.

"I'm married now, and I have two children. My wife doesn't know the old Little Waco. She doesn't fear that I'm going to go out and do something that could potentially get me arrested. She doesn't know the type of person I used to be. She only knows who I am today. She knows I'm a law-abiding citizen, and I have to thank you for that because you showed me that I wasn't a good drug dealer; I was a good at sales."

Once Little Waco understood that he was good at sales, his vision expanded, and he saw other possibilities, which meant he could picture himself making a living that didn't risk sending him back to prison.

I knew just by his circumstances that Little Waco's desired success was to get out of the halfway house and not come back, so through our resource conversation, I had to listen really closely to the resources he had to make that possible.

One of the resources I heard from him was that he was the number one drug dealer in Waco at age 14. On the one hand, I didn't want to congratulate him for that, but on the other hand, it was important that I asked him how he did that.

I knew he must have had resources within him that, if used well, could change his life for the better. Think of Lex Luthor in the Superman comics and movies. Lex Luthor was a super brain who used his intelligence for bad things. But what if he could have flipped that in his head and told himself, "Hey, I have some amazing gifts!"

Little Waco had amazing gifts too. Imagine the leadership skills he had to do what he was doing at 14 years old. All I did was ask him questions that evoked those resources and helped him see himself differently.

If you hope to make a difference in your life, you have to make a difference with what you see in the mirror, and you need to do so in a more positive way.

When Little Waco first came to the halfway house and attended group therapy, he saw a drug dealer when he looked in the mirror, but by the time he left, he saw someone who was good at sales.

That's the power of describing the resources of your desired success.

WHAT COUNTS AS A RESOURCE?

A Closer Look with Adam

People don't often think about their resources, but as they learn to identify them, they'll realize their own capacity for greatness, which they'll need to achieve change. People also tend to carry more doubts than confidence. Examining their resources provides an opportunity for them to present evidence of their greatness.

Elliott could have decided that because Little Waco was a huge drug dealer at age 14, he was doomed. Instead, he decided to feel impressed and curious about how he accomplished such a feat. Little Waco was a bit like Lex Luthor, and Elliott helped him become like Superman.

The best part about resources is that when people identify and claim them, they transform. Likewise, their loved ones are also impacted. Because Little Waco transformed, he made a new life for himself—one that was stable and included a wife and children, one that didn't involve persuading others to buy or sell drugs. Realizing the unilateral reach of his resources was the impetus for all that remarkable change. It gave him the confidence to utilize skills from one area of his life and apply them to another area.

What counts as a resource? Resources are what you carry inside you—the traits, skills, strengths, and qualities that make you great. Essentially, a resource is anything you can do or that you possess within you, especially in relationship to you accomplishing your desired success.

The ability to achieve a feeling, such as love or empathy, can even be thought of as a resource. Why? Because what you want (your desired success) is something you have felt before—remember, you can't crave what you've never tasted—and because you've felt it before, you must have some know-how, some resource, about how to create it again.

If your desired success is peace, you can ask yourself, "When was peace in my life previously? What did I do to make that happen?" Resources don't need to be framed in the past, however. You can just as easily ask yourself, "What are some qualities I have inside me that let me know I am capable of peace?"

Resources have to do with your *internal* relationship with your desired success, what's within you that can help bring the success about.

If I were to ask a woman, "Are you married?" and she answered, "Yes, I'm married to a man named Curtis," Curtis is not the resource; the woman's love for Curtis is the resource—the love that lives inside her—and it's related to the role she fulfills as his wife.

Likewise, when you think of a teacher, his students aren't the resource; his relationship with the word *teacher* is the resource. The fact that he's accepted the role of teacher guides several things he does in his life, and the resource is the fact that he can do those things.

This same teacher could ask himself, "What do my students notice about me that lets them know I'm doing wonderful things to help them?" and "How did I get so good at those things?" and "What did I do to convince them I was good at those things?"

People's brilliance leaks out and shows up everywhere in their lives. The wife and the teacher in the examples above have other roles in their lives, too, and their strengths in one area can help them in all areas. Describing their resources can help illuminate those for them.

If you tend to give the credit to others for your accomplishments, think a little harder to unlock your own resources. For example, let's say a man says, "I have a great friend who helps me achieve things professionally." That's giving the credit to someone else, so he needs to find a way to bring the accomplishment back to himself. He could do that by asking himself, "What is it about *me* that makes my friend so devoted to working with me?" That causes his thinking to shift so he takes ownership of his resources. He might answer, "I guess I'm a good friend."

Remember that resources are a description pathway on the solution focused diamond. The act of describing them in and of itself is transformative. Thinking about your resources isn't meant to be a problem-solving tool; it's meant to instill confidence in you that you can achieve your desired success. That confidence will come naturally as you continue to describe what you're capable of.

By examining your resources, you'll start to experience yourself in a new way. As a therapist and researcher, I've witnessed countless times how clients stop living the script of "bad mom" or "addict" or "depressed person," and they start believing in themselves, which helps them start living a new script, one in which they view themselves in a positive light.

People forget their own greatness. As a result, they don't apply their greatness unilaterally. They take for granted the exceptional skills they possess and view them as ordinary because those skills have become commonplace in their lives. Perhaps they've been exercising those skills for so many years that they no longer recognize them as noteworthy. They believe they're easy.

It's important to be reminded that if you were great enough to achieve what you've already done before, then you can inherently do more great things. When you catch the vision of your capability, you begin to live up to it.

THE MAN WHO DIDN'T DRINK ON TUESDAYS

Diving Deep with Elliott

Your resources are critical to think about because we live in a world where people don't focus on the skills, traits, and qualities that make them uniquely magical.

During my childhood, I'd produced a tape in my head, a recorded loop that told me, "You're not any good" because I'd been told that very thing so many times by my father. I wasn't geared to think about my resources. I didn't think I was uniquely talented. I believed anything I could do, anyone else could do just as well.

As you can imagine, I didn't initially become an adult who thought I was somehow great and able to do amazing things. The human brain does not work that way.

I've witnessed this same pattern in many others. The number of people I've seen over the years who don't take credit for their own successes is remarkable. People tend to accept blame for their problems but not take credit for their successes.

I once worked with a client who struggled with so much overdrinking that his belly was distended and his skin had a yellowish hue. When I asked him about his desired success, he answered, "I need to be clean and sober." He'd made some bad decisions related to drinking, and he was in danger of losing his wife and family.

"When in your life are you the least likely to drink or to drink less?" I asked, rather than asking about why he had a problem of drinking in the first place. I wanted to highlight his strengths instead of his flaws.

"On Tuesdays," he answered. "I tend to not drink as much or even at all on Tuesdays." When I asked him why, he explained, "I'm the assistant coach on my son's baseball team, and they have practice every Tuesday night, so I need to stay sober. That's also important because I drive my son to and from practice on Tuesdays."

"When did you realize that you were capable of making good decisions once a week?" I asked.

He looked at me like I was crazy. "What do you mean?"

"Well, once a week, you make the decision to go to your son's baseball practice, clean and sober, and you participate as any good and loving dad would. When did you realize you were capable of making good decisions once a week? That's pretty frequent."

He sat back in his chair, processing what I'd said. "I didn't think about it that way. I thought everybody would do the same thing I did."

"No, there are lots of stories in the news about people driving drunk while their kids are in the car. Also, people in your position might drink earlier in the day, thinking they can sleep it off in time, but you don't drink at all on Tuesdays."

He rubbed his jaw, mulling that over. "I guess that's true."

"What skills do you draw upon to make Tuesday happen?" I asked.

He started to get emotional when he replied, "Well, I guess I draw upon my skills of being a good dad because those things sound like good dad things, don't they? And if you think about it, making dinner and coaching your son's baseball team and tucking your daughter in bed, like, yeah, those sound like good dad things to me."

"What else?" I asked.

"Well, I guess I use some discipline because I choose not to drink on Tuesdays," he said, and he continued describing all the skills he utilizes to make Tuesdays a nonalcohol day.

"If you walked out of my office and all these resources became a bigger part of you, what would you notice?" I asked.

"I would do this more than just on Tuesdays," he replied.

"How much more?"

"I don't know. I never thought about it before, but I would do it more than just on Tuesdays."

"Well, let's see how much more you can do it. Come back and let me know."

A week later when he returned to therapy, he told me he'd added another day in the week without drinking. This time he hadn't drunk on Tuesday or Wednesday. We talked about how he did that and what resources he drew upon.

The next week, he added Thursday to the mix of nondrinking days. A few weeks later, his wife called and told me he'd done something she'd been trying to get him to do for years—he checked himself into a detox center. He'd reduced his drinking so much that he'd started to have tremors that were concerning and his doctor recommended he be under medical care as he continued to get sober.

He went to the detox center and continued to not drink. I didn't see him again for several months. Then one day he appeared in the lobby of my office, and he looked like a million bucks—healthy, no longer yellow, trimmer, and clean-cut. He told me he hadn't had a drink in six months.

"The thing that helped me reduce my drinking," he said, "wasn't going to AA meetings; it was remembering that somewhere deep inside of me there was a good dad, and I wanted to live my life as a good dad. I went from not drinking on Tuesdays to Wednesdays to Thursdays, and then to only once a week and then to once a month and then eventually to no alcohol at all. And I haven't had any alcohol in six months."

He burst into tears and handed me his six-month sobriety chip. "I want to give you this because I wouldn't have this if it weren't for you." He told me he now coaches his son's baseball team all the time, and he's there for his daughter when she needs him. What helped unlock his ability to move toward his desired success to get sober was remembering he already had a good dad living inside him. His resources to succeed already existed; he just needed to maximize them. Once he realized he could make good decisions once a week, he thought of himself as being capable to make more good decisions.

His sobriety chip remains one of my prized possessions.

LIVE A LIFE BASED ON YOUR RESOURCES, NOT YOUR FLAWS

Diving Deep with Elliott

My colleague, Chris Iveson, likes to say that people are parallel stories: they're both the problem (or living with the problem) and the resources (or living with the resources). Part of the process of unlocking your potential and moving toward your desired success is recognizing that the talents, skills, and traits you need already live inside of you.

The most important thing you can do is to believe in yourself, and the most important component to believing in yourself is being more aware of your talents than your flaws. We all have flaws, but you have to be more aware of what makes you brilliant than what makes you flawed.

When you find and tap into your resources, your flaws become irrelevant to the task at hand. I'm sure they're still relevant to your life and your story, but they're irrelevant to your task of achieving your desired success. You already have all have the skills within you to succeed. This was a lesson I also learned for myself.

Let me tell you who I am. I'm someone who can do hard things. I can drive from Texas to Atlanta overnight with no sleep. I can write a research article, even when I'd never done so before. I can publish a book, even back when everyone, including my professors, told me, "You're too new to write a book." I can also host my own TV show. I know and believe in what I teach like the back of my hand.

How do I know I can do all these things, especially when I hadn't done them the first time around? I didn't let my father's beatings stop me from life's ambitions. What looks on the surface like a flaw in me is actually my greatest strength.

I'm not sorry for my difficult childhood because I learned that I can own the struggle and continue to triumph. My legs are strong, and I can stand up again. There's a quote I love by political activist Reverend Jesse Jackson, whose father was a professional boxer: "The ground is no place for a champion. The ground is no place that I will wallow on." That means you have to get up and keep fighting. Your resources exist within you to keep you in the ring.

One of my favorite movies is *Apollo 13* with Tom Hanks, which is based on a true story of a three-man crew that was supposed be the third group of men to have walked the moon. Instead, an oxygen tank exploded while they orbited the moon, and NASA's Mission Control and the astronauts themselves had to rally together to find a way to return to Earth safely.

As written about on *Looper,* "One of the tensest scenes in the movie comes when the crew realizes that while they're getting plenty of oxygen in their cabin, they don't have a way of filtering out carbon dioxide. If they didn't find a way to filter it out, they would have been in danger of asphyxiation. In a moment that may have felt to audiences like contrived Hollywood dramatization but was actually 100 percent true, the crew realized that the lithium hydroxide canisters that would have easily scrubbed the air in the command module were square and wouldn't fit in the round holes of the lunar module they had to take refuge in. Yes, their task became fitting a square peg into a round hole."[2]

Instead of lamenting over what they didn't have to work with to help the astronauts survive, the ground crew got creative and brainstormed a solution using materials they knew the astronauts would have on hand. Strong people assess their assets. They devised a funnel to redirect the air through the filters from spacesuit hoses, plastic bags, cardboard covers of flight logs, and finally duct tape.

They shared their instructions with the astronauts, who built a copy for themselves in space. In less than an hour, the carbon dioxide levels in their spacecraft dropped to acceptable levels and were no longer a danger for the rest of the mission.

The astronauts of *Apollo 13* were hit hard, just like you'll be hit hard in life, just like I was hit hard. But I don't care how much life has hit you. I don't care how much your father sucks. You still have stuff on your spacecraft that's good. You already have the tools you'll use to accomplish whatever it is you need to accomplish.

Never allow your flaws or shortcomings to distract you from your talents, skills, and traits. They have the full power to keep you living within your purpose and achieving your desired outcome. They're all you need to be unstoppable.

TIPS FOR DISCOVERING YOUR RESOURCES

A Closer Look with Adam

As you complete the worksheet at the end of this chapter, you're going to face perhaps the most difficult task in this book. This worksheet consists of several rows of lines, which are meant for you to list your resources—the skills, characteristics, strengths, talents, and traits you have within you that let you know you can accomplish your desired success.

You may be overwhelmed, thinking, *How am I going to fill in all those blank spaces? Do I really have that many resources that can help me on my journey?* But if you keep digging—keep looking at your life and the things you do, how you spend your time, and examine what loving people know about you—you'll start to realize you have an endless number of resources that you can start to utilize.

As with the previous worksheets in this book, the more specific and detailed you can get, the better. Be sure to complete the entire page. We're very serious about this. Do not move on in the book until you complete it. You'll thank us later. Use the blank page following the worksheet for more room if you need it or if you'd like to add even more resources. Your list can be longer than the space we've provided has allotted for, but it can't be less than it.

Here are a few tips to help you complete the worksheet and uncover all your resources:

Put a label on it: Break down more generalized resources like "I'm a good parent" into the traits, skills, strengths, or qualities that make up that statement. Put a label on each of them. If you use determination to be a good parent, write down "determination." When you put a label on your resource, it will be easier to refer to when you revisit this list. You'll be able to say, "Oh, that's right. I need to use determination" or whatever your resource may be.

Add a description: For every resource you label, add a description. For example, if courage is one of your resources, ask yourself, "What does courage look like? What do I notice to let myself know I'm seeing courage or using courage?" Descriptions of resources help them become more noticeable when you encounter them again in life. The more you notice them, the better you'll become at utilizing them.

Presuppose the best in yourself: As you continue to think of resources to complete your list, it might be helpful to ask yourself questions that include a presupposition—an assumption built into the thing that is present (in this case, a resource).

For example, you could ask, "If I accomplish my desired success, what skill would I have drawn on to do that?" or "What skill would my partner have noticed?" or "What characteristic would my children have seen me use?"

All those questions presuppose the presence of your skills and traits, but they arrive at them from you imagining different people's perspectives about you—those from your partner, your children, your co-workers, and so on. Some resources you might recognize on your own, but you will recognize more as you consider what other people would say about you.

Be sure to presuppose the presence of these resources from the perspective of those who love you because they're the ones who can see things in you that you might overlook or discredit for yourself. Additionally, when you view your resources from someone else's perspective, you have to take ownership of them. You have to say, "Okay, yeah, they must see something that maybe I don't see or that I want to discount about myself." It helps you accept that it's true.

Examine an accomplishment: In the same vein of breaking down more generalized resources into more detailed ones and then putting a label on them, it also helps to think about what resources led you to accomplish something meaningful in your life. To illustrate how this is done, here are some questions Elliott asked our friend Cecil and me during one of the webinars we teach together. You can ask similar questions of yourself.

Elliott: Adam, what is something you've accomplished in your life that you're proud of?

Adam: I got a doctoral degree.

Elliott: What is one skill you drew upon to accomplish that doctoral degree?

Adam: Grit.

Elliott: Okay, so Adam would write "grit" on his list of resources. Now, Cecil, what is one thing you're proud of that you've accomplished?"

Cecil: Finishing college.

Elliott: What's one skill you drew upon to finish college?

Cecil: Hard work when I didn't feel like it.

Elliott: What do you call working hard when you don't feel like it?

Cecil: Effort.

Elliott: Cecil can write down "effort" on his list of resources.

Don't take things for granted: Find gratitude for the smallest, tiniest resources you possess. Don't brush them aside as being worthless. They aren't. They're much more impactful than you realize. That impact is unilateral. Your skills, qualities, and characteristics—resources you've used in one arena of your life—can be utilized in a different arena in a different way.

Become comfortable with pride: We've mentioned this before, but resisting the urge to shout accolades about yourself doesn't serve you well. Instead, embrace the value of owning your strengths and talents—abilities you have that help you uniquely contribute to the world. If you don't understand the qualities you possess, you're not going to be able to live within your purpose to its full extent.

You don't have to be boastful to own your greatness, but you *do* need to identify it, acknowledge it, and claim it. Give yourself permission to be positive about yourself without holding back. Don't minimize your talents. You can't manifest your potential until you claim the full strength of who you are.

Share your discoveries: When you finish completing the list of resources, speak about what you wrote to others. The more you share your desired success, the more it will become a reality. Find supportive people, people who will hold you up, and tell them about the things that stood out to you on your list. Be courageous in declaring your desired success and then utilize your resources to make it happen. Tell your circle of supporters, "This is where I'm headed. Please hold me accountable on the journey."

We encourage you to revisit this list as many times as you can to help remind you of your talents. If we asked you to tell us about your flaws, you'd be able to rattle them off without effort because that's human nature. But this is a list that comprises your brilliance. So get to know it. Be in touch with it. Become fluent in your strengths. Believe in yourself against all odds.

What skills and resources do you possess that can help you achieve this dream?

CHAPTER 14

FUTURE SUCCESS

A Diamond Description Pathway

THE DOPE SICK CLIENT

Diving Deep with Elliott

Early on in my career, a mother called me and said her 19-year-old daughter, Mary (name changed), was addicted to heroin and heavily abusing it. She asked if I could help her get clean.

When Mary came to my office for the first time, I began our session by asking, "What are your best hopes from our talking?" She told me she was a freshman in college, and she wanted to become an attorney. Becoming an attorney was her desired success.

Now imagine someone telling you that they want to become an attorney with track marks all over her arms. I thought, *There is zero chance that this person is going to be an attorney. I'm not even sure she will ever be clean from heroin. How on earth can she expect me to help her with what she wants?*

I admit I wasn't confident when I asked Mary, "What difference would it make for you to become an attorney?"

"I'd be happy," she answered. "It's the job I've always wanted to do since I was a kid."

I so badly wanted to exclaim, "Then get clean from heroin and maybe you'll have a chance!" Instead, I simply said, "Suppose you woke up tomorrow and you were on your way to doing the job you've wanted to do since you were a kid. What would you notice?"

Mary described her future success with me, detailing what it would look like to be on the pathway to becoming an attorney.

We scheduled a follow-up session, and when that time and day came, Mary didn't show up. I thought maybe she was lost. She'd only been to my office once before. I walked into the parking lot to see if any cars were circling the area—maybe I could wave her down—but I still couldn't find her. When I came back into the lobby of my office, I noticed someone was in the women's bathroom. The door was shut, and the bathroom light was shining under the crack of the door.

I waited in the lobby and finally Mary came out of the bathroom, now 25 minutes late for our appointment. She entered my office, and we did a follow-up session that only lasted 20 minutes because that's all the time we had left. That was the last time I saw her.

Mary called me a month later and apologized for being late to our last session. She confessed that she had been shooting up in the bathroom.

Now you might be wondering, *How do you do therapy with someone high on heroin?* Well, if you know anything about heroin, you know that people only get high the first time. They continue using so they don't get dope sick. Mary was using heroin to avoid feeling that way.

She apologized and said, "I'll call you in the future when I need another session."

I didn't hear from her again for about eight years, and then I received an invitation for her law school graduation. It included a handwritten note from her. She told me if that it hadn't been for the sessions I'd done with her, she never would have believed she could become an attorney. And without that hope, she never would have been able to break her addiction.

That was the moment in my career when I realized that these solution focused descriptions do lead toward change. Descriptions aren't about superficial things changing for people; they're about what's foundational and motivational for them, what's in their hearts becoming their realities.

Although I didn't have confidence in Mary's transformation at the beginning of our first session, I pushed past my doubts and trusted her capability, and she went on to construct a meaningful description of her future success. Despite Mary's setback after our first session, hope took root in her, and she changed into the person she wanted to be.

THE IMMEDIACY OF YOUR FUTURE SUCCESS

A Closer Look with Adam

People don't want to change in days, months, or years down the road. They want to change *now*, and they can. As of this moment, they can start living a new reality, one in which their future success is present.

Envisioning that level of immediacy is valuable because it introduces the change that people are seeking. Immediately, they can start noticing signs that the life they are hoping for is present. Immediately, they can start acting on that change. Immediately, they can start behaving consistently with the version of themselves they would like to be.

While immediacy is important, your future success doesn't always have to be right now. Think of Elliott's session with Mary, who was addicted to heroin. She wanted to become an attorney, but she was only a freshman in college. She couldn't have actually become an attorney by the next morning. That's why Elliott asked her questions about a future that could begin tomorrow, but it was also a future about her being *on her way* to becoming an attorney and the difference that would make in her life.

As you complete the worksheet at the end of this chapter, it may be helpful for you to consider the immediacy of your future success being present in your life. What would it look like if you woke up tomorrow, and without knowing how it happened, what you're seeking—or who you want to be—was suddenly present? What would you notice to let you know it was present? What would others notice about you? What difference would that make in your life?

DETAILED DESCRIPTIONS TRIGGER LASTING CHANGE

Diving Deep with Elliott

The more specific a description you can construct about your future success, the more likely you'll change because details are profound for the human brain.

I love to cook, and I remember one time my buddy called and said, "Hey, I want to make dinner for this girl I'm dating, and I like your lasagna. Can you please share the recipe?"

"Sure," I said, and I gave it to him.

He went to the store, got all the ingredients, and called me back again when he was making it. He asked question after question so he could cook it just right. One and a half hours later, by the time I got off the phone after coaching my friend, I was really craving lasagna. Why? My brain had gone through every detail of preparing it.

That's what a detailed description can accomplish for you. If you deeply envision a version of yourself that is sober, it makes you crave sobriety.

I've already told you the story of Mary, the freshman in college who was addicted to heroin. I worked with another woman who also was addicted to heroin, and in our therapy session, I guided her to describe the day she was going to wake up sober. We spent about 40 minutes describing that day in extraordinary detail.

She scheduled another session for two weeks later, and when the time came, she didn't show up. I tried to call her, but her phone was out of service.

A month later, she called and said, "Sorry I missed the session. I was in rehab. I'm out now, and I've been clean for 28 days."

"What happened to help you get clean?" I asked, impressed.

"I just kept thinking of myself as the version I was when I was talking to you," she said. "And when I left your office after our session, the cab driver who came to pick me up asked, 'Where to?' 'Home' felt like the wrong answer because I knew home was where the drugs were. I asked him to take me to the hospital instead. That began my journey of sobriety. Answering those detailed questions with you ignited something in me that I didn't know was there before."

That woman stayed clean for at least two years. I know because I talked to her daughters at that time, and they said she had maintained sobriety.

Remember and believe in the power of description. As you construct the details of your future success and deeply imagine the difference it will make in your life, you will trigger lasting change. You'll transform.

LANGUAGE CREATES REALITY

A Closer Look with Adam

To add to what Elliott just shared, detailed descriptions are transformative because they help your language become tangible, and that tangibility becomes real. Language can truly create reality, and it happens as you describe your future success.

From a neuroscientific perspective, this transformation process can be thought of as neuroplasticity. Human brains are always changing and creating synaptic connections from moment to moment. That, in turn, affects the way people experience and make sense of life events, relationships, and themselves. When you ask yourself solution focused questions to describe that change, you're influencing neuroplasticity in a very powerful and purposeful way.

The description you construct needs to be specific. You will describe things like the day your desired success happens, what it will look like, what will be different about you when it occurs, how you will act, what you will think, what you will eat, what your partner will notice, what your co-workers will notice, what your friends will notice, what your children will notice, what your pet will notice, and so on.

As you describe detail after detail of the change being present, your brain will begin to change, and that change will become reality. It will happen as you write about change, talk about change, think about change, and converse about change.

When you construct that level of a future success description, you will not only realize that pieces of your desired success are often already occurring in your life but also that you already know how to move forward toward achieving what you want in a meaningful way.

PAY ATTENTION TO THE MUSIC, NOT THE RAIN

Diving Deep with Elliott

Adam and I want you to notice the difference in yourself as you move toward your desired success—and that difference should be joy, however that manifests for you.

When I was an eight-year-old kid struggling from abuse, I watched an old movie on TV called *Singing in the Rain.* The main character is played by Gene Kelly, who, in the most iconic scene in the film, tap dances brilliantly in a deluge of rain.

I remember being fascinated and wondering, *How do you learn to pay attention to the music and not the rain?* In other words, how do you learn to pay attention to what inspires you and makes you want to dance and not be impacted by the rain? I believe that comes, in part, by recognizing your brilliance and what brings you joy.

People are more amazing than they give themselves credit for. What they discount as normal behavior is actually exceptional behavior. Even consistent "normal" behavior can be thought of as amazing because how many people struggle with consistency? Many people. Perhaps consistency is your zone of brilliance.

Don't fall into the trap of normalizing your brilliance. What you do matters. Part of the crime of humanity is that people do brilliant things so often that they forget that they're brilliant. I'm so fortunate that in my occupation I get to remind people of their brilliance.

Learn to look at yourself through the lens of brilliance. Every single one of you is brilliant at something. You just need to find your zone and live there, focusing on it, in spite of the turmoil that may be happening around you.

As you complete the worksheet at the end of this chapter, consider what you'll notice differently about yourself as you move toward your desired success and fight past the instinct of "I don't know." Look at yourself with the same loving eyes you'd give to the person you care most about in life, and find the answers through that hope-filled and generous perspective.

Do the same thing as you consider what others would notice about you, which is another question on the worksheet. What's the smallest detail they would see about you to give them a clue that something is different? I promise you, everyone in your life will notice something. Push yourself past any "I don't knows" and think harder. Believe in yourself.

Learn to pay attention to what brings you joy because what you and others should notice differently about yourself is that you're filled with joy. What does joy look like for you? I could tell as a kid watching *Singing in the Rain* that dancing brought Gene Kelly joy. In my case, shooting arrows brings me joy. (I'll share more on that next.) My friendship with Adam also brings me joy. Our Batman-Robin partnership is the result of us living within our purpose.

What lets you know that you're living within your purpose? What brings you joy? How do you notice that difference in you? How does it show up in the smallest ways?

Life doesn't happen by coincidence. Its successes come from being intentional and purposeful. Envisioning the positive differences in yourself as you move toward your desired success is a powerful way to make that happen. When you move with a purpose, you arrive at a better destination.

THE IMPACT OF MY RAMBO HOBBY

Diving Deep with Elliott

Near the end of 2020, I was stressed, not only from the pandemic, but also from the strain of running my business amid the division in the country from the presidential election. I just needed a mental break.

As a child, I'd always loved bow-and-arrow superheroes like Robin Hood, Hawkeye, and Storm Shadow (a G.I. Joe character). As I was sitting in my house one day, I randomly decided, "I'm going to go shop for a compound bow." It felt like the perfect antistressor.

I had never shot with or owned a compound bow. Compound bows were meant for guys like Rambo. But on that day, I thought, "Why not also for me?"

I went to a shop in town that sells compound bows. I'd only ever entered this store once before, and that was 20 years previously. I was a total fish out of water, but one of the workers helped me choose a great beginner's bow. I didn't want to invest too much money because I didn't know if I'd enjoy this new hobby. But the worker assured me that my beginner's bow could be upgraded to an expert bow if I got into this.

That seemed like a fair risk, so for $240 I bought a compound bow, some arrows, and a target. Now I had everything I needed to fulfill my childhood superhero dream of being an archer.

The next day I went out in my yard and started shooting my new bow. If you know anything about me, you know I obsess about things that I want to become good at—and I wanted to get to a point where I could shoot targets with accuracy and hit a bull's-eye.

Jokingly, I told Adam I wanted to shoot an apple off his head, to which he replied, "You'll never see that happen." I promised myself I'd shoot at least 30 arrows every day. At least I'd be working toward that bull's-eye.

I soon discovered that shooting with my compound bow is the most calming thing. When I'm shooting, I can't think about anything else except the actual exercise: my breathing, how I'm standing, my environment, and so on. When I shoot, the world doesn't seem to exist. It's just me, my bow, and my target.

After about a week of shooting, Anna, the chief executive officer of our business, told me, "I've noticed you are less irritable." I hadn't had a hobby for the entirety of my adult professional life. My hobby was getting on airplanes, traveling around the world, and teaching people Solution Focused Brief Therapy. But once I got a real hobby and stayed consistent with it, even for just 20 minutes a day, Anna told me, "Your mood has changed. You seem more joyous."

I started sharing Facebook posts of me shooting my bow, like one where I pop a balloon from 15 yards away with my arrow. Comments came pouring in about how I appeared so happy and how they hadn't seen me look like this in a while. I had a glimmer in my eyes, they said. My smile was infectious. I seemed enthused.

I was surprised to realize how much people pay attention when I didn't think they would. They noticed the impact of what was different about me. My new hobby changed my life for the better, and it also affected their lives. They didn't just notice the change in me but changed as well. Their moods escalated just by seeing my mood escalate.

I also shared recordings of me failing to hit my targets, like the first video I posted, where I miss my target by four feet and my arrow sticks in a fence. Chris Iveson, a colleague and close friend, saw that video and texted me, saying, "You look very happy. I'm glad to see you've gotten a hobby." It almost moved me to tears, reading that. So many people were noticing something transform in my life, even from something as small as my practicing archery. I wasn't even hunting. I was just shooting my target in my backyard for 30 times a day, and it greatly impacted me in a way people noticed.

Think about who will notice the small changes you're making. What would they notice? I wasn't shocked that people close to me saw signs of my transformation, but it surprised me to see that my followers on social media, people I didn't know well, were saying things like, "Something has shifted in you, and we're happy about it."

People were not only noticing the small changes in me, but they also cared enough to tell me what they noticed and how happy they were for me.

You'll experience the same for yourself if you're on the lookout for it. As you make small shifts to get on track with your desired success, I promise those shifts will impact others.

Some of the questions we ask in the worksheet at the end of this chapter are, "Who would be most likely to notice you moving through each day with such purpose?" and "What would they say they're noticing about you?" and "How would they let you know they noticed?" and "Describe what difference it would make for you knowing they'd noticed these things."

Because people are such social beings, they look for and appreciate the validation of others. They aren't completely dependent on this validation, but it can provide motivation, encouragement, and an added sense of purpose. Often your purpose is entwined with important people in your life. Therefore, when you consider what others will notice, you are just acknowledging the difference this support makes to you.

Also, because it can be difficult to completely own your own greatness, imagining what other important people would notice about you and considering what it might mean to them to see you be successful, is often an easier place to start when you contemplate the details of your desired success.

NOTICE EVEN THE SMALLEST DIFFERENCES

A Closer Look with Adam

When my clients come to therapy, I'll ask them, in the context of them envisioning their future success, "What do you notice that's different about you?"

They'll often start by being dismissive. "Oh, I'm just doing my same normal thing," they'll say. "I go to work, come home, take a shower, watch a little TV, and then go to bed."

But there's more to be noticed when you're living within your purpose. And to find it, you need to notice the difference within the ordinary—or in some cases, the difference within the difference, such as when you're doing something new, like Elliott shooting 30 arrows each day with his compound bow.

The deeper you dig for those details of difference, the more transformative the exercise of envisioning your future success will be. You'll live it because you've manifested it in such a specific way.

To help my clients when they are having a hard time finding any differences to notice, I'll choose one of the things they've answered with—something they perceive as mundane—and highlight it in a new way. I might ask them something like, "How will you go to work differently than you did yesterday?" Soon they'll start to break down the smallest shifts in their day, and then meaningful differences will emerge and become noticeable.

I was once conducting therapy for a woman who struggled with anxiety, and she described that feeling as having butterflies in her stomach. Later, when she described the difference it would make to achieve her desired success, she also answered, "I would have butterflies in my stomach."

Even though her descriptions were the same, I knew there must be a difference between anxious butterflies in her stomach and living-in-her-purpose butterflies in her stomach, so I asked, "What's different about these butterflies in your stomach when your desired success is present?"

She was able to then articulate how those butterflies came with an excited feeling, rather than an anxious one.

One of the questions we ask in the upcoming worksheet is, "What would they say they're noticing about you?" In other words, what would people notice about you when you're moving toward your desired success?

The number one answer we get to this is, "They'll notice that I'm smiling." But you can go deeper than that and pull apart the minute differences of that smile. To do that, you can ask yourself a follow-up question: "What would people notice about this smile that would let them know it's a purpose-filled smile rather than an ordinary smile?"

In the same vein, Elliott could have answered that worksheet question by saying, "People will notice I'm shooting arrows now," which is fine, but a more transformative answer will come from him asking, "What would let them know I'm shooting arrows with a purpose in mind?"

MY BROTHER WOULD BE PROUD OF ME

Diving Deep with Elliott

I remember watching the godfather of descriptions, my colleague Chris Iveson, guide a future description with a client during a recorded session. Chris had a flip chart with him, and he wrote numbers 1 through 30 on one of the pages. The client who he was working with was a Black guy in his 20s, and when he saw Chris write down all those numbers, he said, "Oh, I'm not going to be able to come up with 30 things." That's how many details Chris wanted him to describe about his future success being present in his life.

Undeterred, Chris started asking him questions, and despite the client's frustration in the process, he did come up with 30 things. The moment he finished, Chris announced, "Let's see if you can come up with 5 more, and we can get to 35." The man reluctantly did, then Chris said again, "How about five more?"

When Chris asked for the 38th time, "What else would you notice that would let you know that your desired success is becoming your reality?" the man burst into tears and answered, "My older brother would be proud of me."

"What difference would it make for your older brother to be proud of you?" Chris asked gently.

The man wiped his eyes and replied, "Well, my older brother just recently came home from prison, and if he saw me making these changes in my life, he would be proud of me. He wouldn't fear that I'd be going down the same path he did, and he wouldn't feel like a failure as an older brother."

This man seemed shocked by the words coming out of his mouth, but they were true and impactful. He came back to therapy a few months later and told Chris how much that answer about his brother changed his life.

In the worksheet questions at the end of this chapter, you'll notice several lines are provided. They're meant to help you think of answers you've never thought of before, just like Chris guided his client to do by repeating the same question 38 times. Making lists like this will help you manifest your reality by focusing deeply on it by describing answers that lead to profound changes.

THE SWITCHES YOU NEED TO LIGHT ON FIRE

A Closer Look with Adam

A few years ago, when Elliott came to visit me at my house, he brought along his compound bow. "Come and shoot with me," he said, after he got settled in. The last time I'd shot a bow was 30 years previously, when I was a Cub Scout at summer camp, and that was a very simple bow. Elliott's bow was much more complex.

On a compound bow, there's a tiny circle built into the string you pull back called a peep sight, which is a little hole you're supposed to look through to take aim. Then on the front of the bow, there's another circle, a bigger one called the bow sight. As you're taking aim, the goal is to line up the peep sight, the bow sight, and your target.

My left arm is not my dominant arm, so it was a bit shaky when I attempted to shoot Elliott's bow for the first time. As I pulled the string back and tried to line up the sights with my target, I dropped my wrist by just a fraction of a centimeter, and my arrow shot into the ground instead of the target. Because my aim was off by such a tiny difference, it resulted in me missing my target by a foot and a half.

As you work toward your desired success, differences matter, even the slightest ones. Minute differences can either help keep your aim intact or throw you off course. Taking the time to envision those little differences of positive change in your life will help you manifest those changes. You'll notice them when they occur and be able to build upon and maximize them. Likewise, you'll notice the small things that derail you and then be able to course-correct quickly.

Another example that illustrates the importance of small differences is the trains in Chicago. When I lived there, every day I would ride the train from the suburbs to the city. On that daily journey, the train would encounter a place where its employees would have to move what they called the switch—the place where the train could change route by switching tracks.

Chicago is very cold in the winter, so sometimes the switch would freeze and be unable to move. This happened one day as my train was coming into the station. It came to an abrupt stop that shocked all the commuters on board. We soon realized we'd stopped because the switch ahead had frozen over, and if we'd kept going without switching tracks, we would have missed the stop at our station and ended up in the next state over. That small point of the switch, in comparison to the miles and miles of tracks around Chicago, was critical to keep us on route.

To thaw the switch, train employees lit the tracks on fire, which seems like a bizarre thing to do, but in Chicago it's common practice. The trains regularly run on top of lit tracks to keep the switches moveable. Normally trains don't have to stop, but mine did because the tracks had suddenly frozen and were not yet on fire. Once they lit them up, the switch was able to reroute the tracks to our appropriate destination.

As you complete the worksheet at the end of this chapter, we ask you the question, "What do you hope you will see yourself doing that would let you know you are moving toward your desired success?" As you write down your answers (several lines are provided), be sure to take note of all the seemingly small things you envision doing or being because they have the power to bring about a great difference in your life.

For example, there's difference between positivity and optimism. Optimism is something that's within you, something you can control and maneuver. It might show itself as positivity, but you don't want to fake positivity. You want to feel genuinely optimistic. Perhaps changing from someone who only shows positivity to someone who also feels it is a switch you need to light on fire.

Pay attention to the smallest details as you envision your future success and find the courage to ignite them into action. Look for the switches you need to light on fire, the little shifts you need to make to ensure you're living within your purpose and arriving at the destination of your desired success.

THE DIFFERENCE OF AUTHENTICITY

Diving Deep with Elliott

I like to think of myself as a self-aware, authentic person, but when I first started working with Adam, I found myself in environments that were new and made me uncomfortable, such as professional conferences. I used to call Adam and ask, "What are you going to wear?"

And he'd answer with something like, "Tan slacks, brown shoes, and a button-up shirt and tie."

This is hard to admit, but I used to try to dress like him because I thought that must be the uniform of academic professional success.

But it didn't work for me. It impacted my ability to be successful and feel happy and comfortable in my own skin.

Through my journey of growing up and not feeling successful or happy, I knew I couldn't do that any longer and I just had to be myself. One of the hardest things in the world is to show up as your true self.

That was especially hard as a Black person, knowing not many people would look like me as I showed up in professional spaces. I knew I would get criticized, judged, and called unprofessional when I dressed the way I wanted to. But I had to get over that and realize that true acceptance would only come if I could be authentically me.

I promised Adam that I'm always going to be me because he and I are at our best when I'm me and he's him. That means he shouldn't put on Jordan brand sweatsuits like I do because that's not him. That also means I shouldn't wear slacks and a dress shirt and tie because that's not me. We have to be who we are. That's where we find our power, our freedom, and our success.

I can't succeed if I'm not being me. I can't ask people to love me, appreciate me, follow me, and buy into what I'm saying if I don't show who I am. That was a hard thing to learn and an even harder thing to do, but now I live by it. Now I can say, "This is me in my culture. This is me in my personhood. This is truly me in every way." And now when I experience success, I can own it because I'm me as I accomplish it.

As simple as it seems, my first step in achieving my desired success—becoming someone who can change the world through love—was owning the way I dress. I don't call Adam and ask him what I should wear anymore. And I don't worry what other people think of me. I trust that they will come to accept that this is authentically me in my sweatsuits and Air Jordans.

A few years ago I got invited to do a keynote at a conference hosted by the Harvard School of Medicine, and what made that especially awesome is that they didn't ask the façade of Elliott to come and speak. They asked the real Elliott to come and speak because that's who they knew me to be; that's all I had ever showed them.

To achieve your desired success, you don't necessarily need to make huge changes in your life to experience a meaningful transformation. For me, great impact came just from embracing the wardrobe I feel comfortable in.

What small changes can you make in your life that will result in a meaningful difference for the better?

YOU ARE THE ARCHITECT OF YOUR OWN LIFE

A Closer Look with Adam

You are at the very beginning of making an impactful change in your life, and that is so important and valuable, but it's going to require effort and energy. Completing the following worksheet will help. It contains a series of questions to guide you in pulling apart the differences that you and others will notice when you're moving toward your desired success—in other words, when signs of your future success are present.

If you have a hard time answering these questions, that's a good indicator that they are meaningful and require some thought. Solution focused questions are difference oriented, which means they're change oriented. And because they're about change, you're going to have to articulate something in a way you've never done before, which in turn means you are starting to create change in this very moment.

Don't be alarmed if you're stumped for a minute and thinking you don't know. Trust your capability to describe in rich detail what you want. If you don't have a canned, carbon copy, ready-to-go answer, it's because you've never considered this kind of question before, this new kind of reality for yourself.

Once you do, you'll remember your description. It will impact you and foster change. You are the architect and expert of your own life. Respect the knowledge you have within you. Trust it's there and will reveal answers if you don't give up trying.

As you move through each upcoming day, what do you hope you will see yourself doing that would let you know you are moving toward your desired success?

Who would be most likely to notice you moving through each day with such purpose?

What would they say they're noticing about you?

How would they let you know they noticed?

What else?

What else?

Describe what difference it would make for you knowing they'd noticed these things.

CHAPTER 15

ANTICIPATE YOUR OBSTACLES

HAVING A PURPOSE IS DECIDING NOT TO QUIT

Diving Deep with Elliott

I promise that as you move toward your desired success, life is going to throw curveballs at you. You will face obstacles, but you can still come out on top. You're tougher than you realize. You've been knocked down before, but you've gotten back up. You've got a little bit of Rocky in you, and you can take the punches. The best way to be able to do that is to be ready for them. You may not know what struggles are coming, but they're coming. Prepare yourself by drawing on the evidence of your strength.

At one of the conferences I was lecturing at, someone in the audience asked, "How do you overcome hard things?"

I replied, "By deciding to."

All of you embody that same determination. In some sense, your purpose is also a decision you've made. It's you saying, "This is how I'm going to respond to the curveballs."

Maybe the world will throw another pandemic at you. Maybe the economy will crash again. But you will have already decided what you're going to do, no matter what obstacles come. You won't quit or lie down. You'll fight back. You'll keep living according to your purpose. That is strength. It's knowing you can do hard things, like Adam's wife, Becca. She knew she could do hard things when she learned she was diagnosed with cancer. She had been through tough times before, so she knew how to fight and persevere.

I've told you how important and beloved my grandmother is to me. She was a strong and powerful woman. Back when I completed my master's degree, I told her I wanted to write a book, which was a step that would make me very visible in the field of psychotherapy.

In her wisdom, she knew I would face racism, but her belief in me was stronger than her fear. When I'd gotten my first book contract, she pulled me aside and said something I'll never forget: "No matter what, don't you quit. I don't care how hard it gets. I don't care what people say or do; you cannot quit." My grandma's grandparents were born into slavery, and she told me, "You have their blood in you. You cannot quit."

If my grandmother were alive right now, I'd be proud to tell her I didn't quit; I was smart enough to surround myself with people who wouldn't let me. I also foresaw my obstacles. I decided in advance that, no matter what, I'd just keep going.

It's easy to keep that promise to my grandma on days when the sun is shining and everything's going really well. But it's harder to do so on a day when an obstacle is just knocking me over. But days like that are the ones I'm most proud of because that's when I know my grandmother is looking down on me and saying, "The world is testing Elliott, and he is standing up to the world."

When I first showed up in my field, I didn't see a whole lot of people that looked like me, dressed like me, or acted like me, but I was just so excited about being able to practice Solution Focused Brief

Therapy and make a difference in the lives of my clients. I worked hard at it and became one of the best SFBT leaders in the world.

As I built a following and people began to buy my books, awful racism became directed at me from people I didn't know, just like my grandmother predicted. People said they didn't want me lecturing at their conference, and they wouldn't cite my books in their works or use them in their classrooms. It hurt me deeply to my core.

But I also realized I couldn't let those obstacles stop me. I had to let them make me stronger. In 2022, I was subjected to a significant racist attack and was no longer willing to tolerate it, so I pushed back. Now it's one of the proudest moments of my life that I could stand up to it and say, "This is not going to fly. I'm going to call out racism whenever I see it." That made a lot of people upset, but I didn't care because it was my truth, and I needed to defend it.

Some people are not going to be excited when you accomplish your desired success, and you need to be prepared for that hurdle. You need to overcome it. As you experience cycles of obstacle-fight-defeat, take them as signs of your strength and resilience.

Anticipating an obstacle doesn't mean you're on the lookout for everything that can go wrong in your life. It just means you realize that not everyone's going to be thrilled when you experience success. By being aware of that inevitability, your muscles will be flexed and ready to persevere.

In terms of transformation, obstacles come in the form of judgment, oppression, and others trying to limit your opportunities. But you have to make yourself immune to those hardships. You can't always anticipate the attacks and the attackers, but you can devalue them. You do that through loving eyes for yourself because they give you strength. You do that through purpose because it gives you meaning.

I invite obstacles in my life now because they allow me to show my grandmother I'm not going to quit. That strength makes the challenges feel irrelevant to me, nothing to fear. When I look to the future, I have one of two thoughts: excitement or a "bring it on" attitude. That's a decision I've made in advance, and a decision I live by.

THE EXTRA WEIGHT THAT MAKES YOU STRONGER

A Closer Look with Adam

In this chapter, we're asking you to foresee obstacles when they are often unforeseen. But when they do present themselves, that's when your strength shines. That's when your purpose is most noticeable.

I used to be a thin person, and I've put on a few pounds in recent years. Back when I was teaching undergraduates, one of my students said, referring to himself, "I got to get back skinny." That's now my phrase that I keep telling Elliott: "I got to get back skinny."

He and I have been holding an event called Purpose every January since 2021, and one year, before I drove to Texas, where our headquarters was for virtually hosting the event, I made sure to pack my dumbbells. I knew the trip could be an obstacle to my morning workout routine, and I didn't want to break the habit or I might stop doing it altogether.

Each morning in Texas, I got up and used those stupid dumbbells. You already know by now how much I hate working out. It's the worst part of my day. But I've got to get back skinny. I've got to be in good shape to be the best dad to my kids and the best husband to my wife.

The dumbbells are an extra weight I have to carry. They're an obstacle. They make what I already have to do in my workout even harder. If I put the dumbbells down, my immediate life becomes easier. But that extra weight, that extra obstacle, is actually what's most beneficial to me in the long run. If I did the same workout without dumbbells, it would take longer for me to get back skinny. The dumbbells make me stronger.

What might you encounter that is an extra weight, the dumbbells you have to lug around from Georgia to Texas to live according to your purpose? What might you have to lift that's actually going to help you fulfill your desired success? When will your purpose shine most brightly as you overcome the obstacles in your way?

WHEN LIFE RAINS ON YOUR DESIRED SUCCESS

Diving Deep with Elliott

One of the most important lessons I've learned about obstacles happened early on in my career when I was watching a demonstration on Solution Focused Brief Therapy. Up until then, I was certain that anything to do with solution focused work had to stay centered on hope and optimism. But when I went to England and watched my colleague, Chris Iveson, conduct a therapy session, he brought up things that weren't hopeful and optimistic.

Chris's client was a man who said his desired success was to be happy. He shared how anxious and depressed he was and how life wasn't working out the way he wanted.

Chris said to him, "Suppose a miracle happens and you wake up tomorrow and you're happy. What would you notice?"

The client thought about it and answered, "The sun would be shining, there would be no traffic on my way to work, and I would have a parking space close to the front door of my office building. It would just be a wonderful day."

Chris responded with something that shocked me: "Let's imagine that you wake up happy, but on this day the sun is hidden behind the darkest clouds, and as you're on your way to your office, you're stuck in the thickest London traffic you've ever been in. When you finally arrive at your office building, the only parking spot available is one that's the farthest away from the door you need to go in, and as you're walking from your car to that door, it starts to pour rain. How would you notice that you were still happy?"

What is happening? I thought as I heard him say that. Why was a solution focused therapist intentionally throwing obstacles at his client? We were supposed to help clients to *not* dwell on problems.

I later bumped into Chris and asked, "What was that all about?"

His reply blew my mind: "In Solution Focused Brief Therapy, we are not trying to force our clients to be optimistic, positive, and hopeful. We're preparing our clients for the real world, and the real world has obstacles in it. But that doesn't mean you can't still have your desired success."

In other words, despite any external contingencies that life will throw at you, your desired success is still achievable. And it has an even greater chance of being when you're prepared for the obstacles.

Imagine *you're* the one stuck in traffic, the sun is hidden behind the darkest clouds you've ever seen, and as you're walking to the front door of your office—the longest walk you've taken from a parking spot before—it starts to pour rain. How would you notice that you could still be living according to your purpose and moving toward your desired success?

Desired success isn't about everything in your life being good. Instead, it's about you being who you want to be no matter what else is happening around you. Living within your purpose isn't contingent upon the outside world.

In many ways, 2020 was a hard year because of the pandemic and its reverberations. But in other ways, it was one of the best years of my life. Things happened that I'll never forget in the most positive of ways. And that only happened because Adam and I recognized that we could have our desired success in spite of global obstacles. We had to be honest about the challenges. We couldn't pretend they didn't exist. But we could still find a way to succeed with what we do and who we are.

You will always have hurdles, but remember you have the strength to leap them.

GEARING UP FOR THE CHALLENGE

A Closer Look with Adam

All of us will have hurdles as we move toward our desired success, and that's what the following worksheet is going to help you examine. More importantly, it will help you articulate what you know about yourself that you can draw upon to overcome those hurdles.

Your best defense against obstacles is using skills you've already employed before. The resources that have helped you overcome hard things in the past, like the resources my wife took the time to remember and draw strength from after she was diagnosed with cancer.

At the end of the resources chapter (Chapter 13), you came up with a list of skills, talents, and characteristics that already exist in your tool belt. Some of those same answers might return to you as you answer the following questions about obstacles. I hope you uncover even more resources about yourself. You can do so the deeper you dig and more specific you are because what it takes to overcome an obstacle might be something you weren't paying attention to before.

As far as the hurdles go, you'll probably initially think of more general obstacles, but I encourage you to take more time and see if you can get more detailed. Doing so will help you to be able to identify exactly what you need to overcome that challenge. You may discover that an untapped resource is your antidote.

After you complete the worksheet, think about what pleased you the most in your answers. What was at least one new thing you discovered that you had in you that you hadn't already listed on previous worksheets?

Anything worth having is something also worth working hard for, and that difficulty can be reduced as you anticipate and gear up for the challenge. Don't forget you're a fighter. You've done hard things before. Any obstacle that comes your way is just one more thing you're already equipped to deal with.

What hurdles do you imagine may be in your way as you move toward your desired success?

____

____

____

____

And what do you already know about yourself that lets you know you can overcome these hurdles?

CHAPTER 16

CELEBRATION

The Bottom Point of the Diamond

"CONGRATULATIONS, ELLIOTT! YOU PASSED!"

Diving Deep with Elliott

When you actually have success, what are you going to do? We hope you celebrate it! That is why the last point of the diamond is celebration. People who are successful anticipate success. They plan for it. They set the intention. And when success happens, they celebrate it.

I learned an important lesson about celebrating my desired success when I was studying for my exam to become a licensed professional counselor (LPC). I was in the first graduating class of Texas Wesleyan University's counseling program, and there were nine of us who graduated. We then needed to take the LPC exam, and I was super nervous about it. I'd never taken a test with such high stakes before.

When you pass this test, you're a counselor, but if you don't pass it, you've wasted three years of your life and $50,000 in obtaining your master's degree in counseling. Why? You can't go on to practice if you don't have a license.

Some of my peers were so nervous about the test that they didn't tell anyone which day they were scheduled to take it. They were afraid of failing and then having to tell people. But I did the exact opposite. I didn't want keep my testing day a secret. I wanted to prepare for success, so I started telling everyone about it.

When I was a kid, my family didn't have much money, but somehow on every birthday, my mom would manage to buy me a Carvel ice cream cake, which is my favorite ice cream in the world. I found a Carvel Ice Cream Shoppe in the next city over, and a few days before the day of my test, I bought myself an ice cream cake. I had Carvel write on top, "Congratulations Elliott! You passed!"

I was doing an internship at an agency at the time, and I told everyone, "Guess what? I'm passing the LPC later this week, and we are going to eat this to celebrate! Don't touch this ice cream cake until after I pass."

I studied so hard. I'd been studying for months. I didn't want to look foolish in front of everyone, and I wanted to become a psychotherapist so much.

I deliberately chose my birthday as the day I'd take the exam. My peers were worried and said to me, "What if you fail and have a bad birthday?"

"I won't," I assured them. "I'm giving myself the gift of passing an exam."

The cake and my declaration that I'd pass were all to prepare my brain to succeed. And I did succeed. I passed the exam. I was officially a psychotherapist. My co-workers and I ate the ice cream cake, and I had a wonderful birthday.

One of the best ways to prepare your brain for success is to plan a celebration. In doing so, you're much more likely to succeed. Of the nine people in my graduating class who took the licensing exam, the ones who struggled the most, including a few who failed, were those who kept secret what they were doing.

But I, along with my best friend and a few others, embraced the opportunity. This was a big and scary test, but we planned on winning. And those of us who did plan to win crushed the test.

It's surprising how often people don't plan to succeed. Instead, they plan to not fail.

When I was growing up, I played baseball, and one of the things I used to do every time I'd go to bat would be to say this mantra, which was more like a prayer: "Please let me not strike out." But then I realized my goal wasn't to not strike out. My goal was to get a home run. I switched up my mantra and said, "Please let me get a hit."

Don't try to not fail. Plan to win. Plan to be successful. Planning to not fail and planning to win are two different mindsets, and they generate two very different results.

How are you going to prepare your brain for success? How will you plan to win? How will you celebrate? How will you acknowledge that you've achieved the greatness you intended to?

PRACTICE CUTTING DOWN THE NETS

Diving Deep with Elliott

There was a famous basketball coach named Jim Valvano who coached the North Carolina State Wolfpack to a championship in the 1983 NCAA tournament against improbable odds. The Wolfpack weren't the most talented college basketball team. The greatest team was the University of Houston Cougars. But the Wolfpack beat them, thanks to Jim Valvano's coaching.

How did he prepare his team to be champions? He had them practice cutting down the nets.

If you've ever watched a championship celebration in basketball, you know that the winning team brings out a ladder, climbs it, and cuts down the basketball nets so their players can have pieces of it as souvenirs. Hundreds of schools start out playing in the season, but only one school gets to cut down the nets.

According to Thurl Bailey, a Wolfpack player at the time, Jim Valvano brought a ladder to one of their first practices and made everyone simulate a national championship celebration by cutting down the nets, and they practiced for hours.

"It was the most awkward thing that any of us had ever experienced," Bailey said. "I mean, who sits at a 12,000-seat arena with their team and a ladder and asks them to pretend like they're winning a national championship? [Valvano] said: 'What would you do, Thurl, if you won the national championship? How would you act? Would you scream and yell? Would you holler? What would you do?'

"It took us a few times to really get into it, but he wanted us to project ourselves into a national championship because he thought it would give us a sense of bringing us closer to the goal . . . . He was a visionary for sure."[1]

Several months later, the Wolfpack cut down the nets, this time as champions after beating the best team in college basketball. When you start to plan your success, your brain and your actions get in line. Champions anticipate success, and they succeed.

In 1983, the NC Wolfpack were unlikely champions, but Coach Valvano had given them the confidence and belief that they were capable of winning. He had them cut down the nets before they did win, so they knew they could do it. In a real way, they already had.

How can you practice celebrating the achievement of your desired success? How can you prime your brain to be a champion?

CELEBRATING THE GOOD TIMES AND THE HARD TIMES

A Closer Look with Adam

As you begin your journey toward your desired success, among all the excitement and anticipation, there can also be some nervousness and trepidation.

When my wife, Becca, was undergoing chemotherapy treatments for breast cancer, her hair started to fall out. Up until then,

I'd never seen her hair shorter than her shoulders. She very much identified as a person who had long hair. Anticipating that loss was something difficult for her.

To help, one of her friends shared an original poem that was written for her, and that poem was called, "Courage." Part of it reads:

Some people want cars
Flashy speed
Some want islands
All their own
Some just want
Ice cream
But me
I want
The strength
To laugh at fear
I want
The step
I have to take
And I want
These shoulders
To throw back
As I lean forward
And do that thing
I have been avoiding
For so long
And yes
I'll take some ice cream
Too.

In anticipation of the day that my wife was going to have to shave her head, our family went out and brought home four cartons of ice cream in different flavors. As I shaved Becca's head, she cried and I cried, but we also ate ice cream through the experience.

That day could have been horrible and awful, but instead it turned into something special. We started to laugh and enjoy our ice cream together.

After she finished chemotherapy, she needed to complete radiation treatments, and we anticipated when her last day of radiation would come. "No matter what," she told me, "on the last day of radiation, we have to have ice cream."

That day arrived on December 3. We checked our children out of school, Elliott came into town, and we all went with Becca to her last day of radiation. On the way home, we got ice cream. On every December 3, we celebrate with ice cream.

Becca and I look back at what could have been a very difficult time for us and our kids, but in the end it became life-changing for the better. Now we celebrate that success with ice cream. We relish the time we got to spend together and how we grew closer than we ever thought possible.

As you begin your journey of transformation, make sure you plan celebrations throughout. They will help you look forward to milestones of success. Amid all the trepidation of wanting to accomplish something impactful, you need courage. In this book, you've completed worksheets that have outlined everything you need to do. Now plan your celebration with whatever your ice cream is.

IT'S OKAY TO BE PROUD

Diving Deep with Elliott

Despite how much Adam and I encourage others to become comfortable with pride, many people can't get past the mental block of imagining feeling proud of themselves. It goes against the humility ingrained in their culture. They can't stop associating pride with boastfulness. But to understand success, you need to wrap your mind around the idea of pride.

Pride doesn't mean "better than others." Instead, think of pride in terms of being proud of yourself for doing something." What meal would you be proud to cook for someone? What song would you be proud to sing for a group of people? What would you be proud to demonstrate?

Try to connect the feeling of pride with a trait you have because just feeling enthusiastic or joyful about something doesn't connect it directly to your accomplishment. In some sense, you're distancing yourself from what you've done. Instead, find a word that positively connects what you've achieved to what you have inside of yourself. *Honored* is a good example because, like the word *proud*, it conveys that you're good at something.

It's important to claim your contribution toward success because the world is extremely critical. You need to counter that negativity by owning your goodness—not in a boastful or "better than" way, but in a way that helps you claim your talents, skills, and characteristics. Owning who you are is part of accomplishing the full scope of your desired success.

Let's say you're great at basketball. By declaring that, it doesn't mean you're simultaneously saying that someone else isn't also great. You're just owning your own strength.

This topic is personal and important to me because for a lot of my life, many people have overtly told me, "You're a piece of shit." I spent a lot of my adolescent years suicidal because I thought that was true. Part of why my psyche as an adult man can now be held together is that I happen to believe that's *not* true. I do that by recognizing that I *do* have talent, and it's okay to claim it. There's nothing wrong with me saying, "I'm good at this. Maybe I'm not good at *that*, but I'm really good at *this*."

Stop beating yourself up by trying to counteract feelings of not wanting to be proud or boastful. That is going too far. Find ways—and find words—to claim your greatness.

Be proud of yourself, even if no one else is. No one knows how hard you had to fight to get to where you are. No one knows the journey you had to go on to get there. Therefore, no one's going to give you the praise you actually deserve. You have to give it to yourself.

You deserve so much credit for all that you've endured and accomplished, so take a moment to just be proud of you because you are truly amazing. The more you wait for the world to tell you that, the more you'll be disappointed. The world doesn't know your whole journey. But you do. You were there the whole time. Give yourself praise as you celebrate the milestones of your desired success and walk in your greatness because you are remarkable.

MY SURPRISE GRADUATION CELEBRATION

A Closer Look with Adam

In August 2009, I finished my doctoral degree, but there wasn't a graduation ceremony until that December. I got a job in the meantime and moved to Chicago. When December rolled around, I traveled back to Texas to participate in the ceremony. I didn't put much planning into it because I was busy transitioning and getting a new job. I knew my parents would be coming from Utah, but that's all I had prepared for.

I woke up on the morning of my graduation to find out that more than just my parents had arrived. All four of my siblings were also there and had come from all over the country. My sister came from Virginia, and my brother flew from Seattle to Utah, where he met up with my other brother and sister, and they all drove through the night to come to Texas.

All this was a huge surprise. I had no idea they had planned this.

My graduation happened on December 19, six days before Christmas, so we also had an early Christmas celebration together, which they also had planned. All my siblings are married and have children, like me, but they left their families behind to spend some extra special time with me and my immediate family.

My siblings brought the stockings we had when we were children, which I hadn't seen for 10 years, and they also brought a bunch of ridiculous gifts that also hearkened back to our childhood. I treasure the picture we took together, all five of us sitting on a couch and holding our old stockings.

Now, when I look back on the day that I graduated with my doctoral degree, receiving my diploma wasn't the thing that was most important. Spending time with my parents and four siblings was. Although I didn't plan the celebration, if I ever planned another one, it would look just like that one.

As you take the time to consider your celebration, consider what will be most meaningful to you. Who do you want to be there? What will you do together?

The milestones you reach as you work toward your desired success might not be as definitive as a graduation ceremony. You might not have a clear day when you "arrive" at becoming who you want to be. It helps to break apart your journey into smaller milestones that you can celebrate, little achievements you can be proud of that will give you momentum to keep traveling on your path toward success.

A CELEBRATORY WORKSHEET

A Closer Look with Adam

On the following worksheet, we want you to envision the celebration of your desired success as well as what you'll notice to let you know that you've reached an important milestone along the way. As with previous worksheets, there are several "what else" questions with many lines to describe what you hope others will also notice.

You know the drill by now: the more detailed and specific you can get, the more your language will become your reality. Additionally, the more you can identify "what else," the more you'll have to celebrate. To that end, imagine we're asking you many more times, "What else?"

When it comes to what others will notice, remember that this question is different from previous iterations in this book. Instead of asking what others will notice as you move toward your desired success, we're asking what they'll notice now that your desired success is fully formed.

Another question on the worksheet examines what you'll be most proud of. We want you to take stock of all your accomplishments, so be sure to answer it, even if you feel a little uncomfortable with pride. What you're doing is taking stock of all the resources you have within you and noting how they'll help you achieve your success. That's something you shouldn't take for granted. As Elliott put it earlier, you're claiming who you are.

Lastly, we want you to visualize your celebration! You've crossed the finish line of your journey—or one important stage of it—and now you need to mark the moment. What is the most meaningful part of how you'll celebrate? By imagining your celebration, you're practicing "cutting down the nets" like Jim Valvano's Wolfpack. You're priming your brain for future success. You're planning on doing what champions do.

Imagine it's one year from today. What would you notice that lets you know you have achieved an important milestone toward your desired success?

What else?

____

____

____

____

What else?

____

____

____

____

What do you hope others will notice about you as your success is achieved?

1. ____
2. ____
3. ____
4. ____
5. ____
6. ____
7. ____
8. ____
9. ____
10. ____

At your celebration, what do you imagine you'll be most proud of as you look back over your journey? What else?

What else?

What else?

What else?

What else?

Visualize your celebration once you achieve the success you desire. What does it look like?

Write it down and plan your celebration. Remember to be very specific.

What would be the most wonderful part about the celebration and why?

____

____

____

____

____

Optional: Draw your celebration in the space below.

ENCOURAGEMENT FOR THE JOURNEY

Diving Deep with Elliott

My favorite word I've learned by traveling the world is the Zulu word *ubuntu*. It means "I am because you are." What Adam and I do only matters because you show up and gift us with your time and attention. Thank you for reading this book. You are part of making our dreams come true, and that is something we will never take for granted.

Each of us has a dragon lurking in our futures. We're bound to get bad news or hit a stumbling block from time to time. But I hope that by reading this book, you've learned that there is a dragon slayer inside you. And there's nothing any dragon can do that you're not prepared for.

Not everything is going to be sunshine and rainbows for you, but even triumphing over one obstacle is worth celebrating.

Did you know that cancer care centers plan celebrations? Patients ring a bell on the last day of their chemotherapy. I was there with Adam and his kids when Becca rang her bell on her final day, after she'd gone through one of the most difficult things I've ever seen anyone go through.

You won't be able to prevent the hurdles and challenges coming your way, but for every fire-breathing dragon, the dragon slayer in you will be ready. And those defeats are worth celebrating.

Go forward with purpose. Make the next stage of your life the best one. Spread love and kindness as you pursue your desired success. No change for the better is too small or insignificant. Every improvement, no matter the size, is monumental and impactful—not only for you, but also for others in your life. The ripples will keep spreading outward.

Love and positivity are stronger than hate and divisiveness. You are. You're a champion. Be that best version of you always. Your capability is limitless.

CONCLUSION

By now I (Elliott) am hoping you realize that if you want to change your life, you have to change the questions you ask yourself. Many people stay stuck in the problem because they spend time focused on the problem and haven't yet mastered the art of asking themselves better questions. Now, after completing this book, you have gained that mastery as we have shared question examples and the thinking behind the questions. We hope the stories within this book from our lives and from our work help you change your life.

Because I can't help myself, I just have one more story. I was recently lecturing at a conference where one of the attendees asked me to help her overcome an eating disorder. When I said I couldn't help her with that, she was stunned. I explained the reason I couldn't help her was because she was asking herself the wrong question. I further explained that instead of asking how to stop suffering with an eating disorder, which was the question she was asking, she should instead ask who she wanted to be in 10 years. She was moved to tears as I asked her a few questions that shifted her focus from her problem to how she wanted to live during the next 10 years. Did you catch that? The shift from the problem to LIVING! The conversation with this attendee lasted approximately five minutes but clearly had a huge impact on her life as she later came and told me that the short conversation we had made a bigger difference than years of therapy she attended to try to fix this problem. That's exactly what we hope this book did for you!

ENDNOTES

Chapter 1.

1. Kobe Bryant, interview with Alex Rodriguez and Big Cat, The Corp, podcast video, December 31, 2018, https://www.youtube.com/watch?v=ndGZU2BwAVY.

2. Howard Beck, "James Wiseman Is in a Golden State of Mind: 'Whatever It Takes,'" *Sports Illustrated*, October 21, 2022, https://www.si.com/nba/2022/10/21/james-wiseman-warriors-daily-cover.

Chapter 3.

1. Shawn "Jay-Z" Carter, Jelani Cobb, "The Shawn Jay-Z Carter Lecture Series," (lecture, Columbia University, New York, NY, February 4, 2020).

2. Chris Drosehn, "Gary Lee and the New York Jets," Overtime Heroics, February 8, 2022, www.overtimeheroics.net/2022/08/02/gary-vee-new-york-jets/.

3. Gary Vaynerchuk, "I Don't Care If I End up Buying the New York Jets," GaryVaynerchuk.com, October 29, 2014. https://garyvaynerchuk.com/i-dont-care-if-i-end-up-buying-the-new-york-jets/.

Chapter 5.

1. Melissa Chan, "Here's How Winning the Lottery Makes You Miserable," *TIME*, January 12, 2016, https://time.com/4176128/powerball-jackpot-lottery-winners/.

2. Erica R. Hendry, "7 Epic Fails Brought to You by the Genius Mind of Thomas Edison," *Smithsonian* Magazine, November 20, 2013, https://www.smithsonianmag.com/innovation/7-epic-fails-brought-to-you-by-the-genius-mind-of-thomas-edison-180947786/.

3. "Famous Quotations from Thomas Edison," Thomas A. Edison Innovation Foundation, https://www.thomasedison.org/edison-quotes.

Chapter 8.

1. Justin Curto, "Jay-Z and Meek Mill Agree They 'Could Never Beef,'" Vulture, August 26, 2022, https://www.vulture.com/2022/08/jay-z-meek-mill-dj-khaled-god-did-verse.html.

Chapter 9.

1. The editors of the Encyclopaedia Britannica, "How a Rejected Block of Marble Became the World's Most Famous Statue," Britannica, https://www.britannica.com/story/how-a-rejected-block-of-marble-became-the-worlds-most-famous-statue.

2. "Quotes of Michelangelo," Michelangelo.org, https://nilsaparker.medium.com/the-angel-in-the-marble-f7aa43f333dc.

3. "Lone Survivor (2014)," History vs Hollywood, https://www.historyvshollywood.com/reelfaces/lone-survivor.php.

4. "Marcus Luttrell 'DRAW A LINE,'" YouTube, uploaded by Rainmaker, August 5, 2016, https://www.youtube.com/watch?v=qGxOYWRAjXQ.

5. *Lone Survivor*, directed and written by Peter Berg, performance by Mark Wahlberg, Universal Pictures, 2013.

Chapter 13.

1. "Jesse Jackson Plans to Return to Public Life," *The New York Times*, January 21, 2001, www.nytimes.com/2001/01/21/us/jesse-jackson-plans-return-to-public-life.html.

2. Keegan McGuire, "Is the Apollo 13 Movie Accurate to the True Story?" Looper, February 19, 2021, www.looper.com/337566/is-the-apollo-13-movie-accurate-to-the-true-story/.

Chapter 16.

1. Jack Dougherty, "Thurl Bailey Remembers the Exact Moment Jim Valvano Won Over the 'Survive and Advance' NC State Wolfpack," Sportscasting, April 3, 2022, www.sportscasting.com/thurl-bailey-remembers-exactmoment-jim-valvano-won-over-survive-advance-nc-state-wolfpack/.

INDEX

Q

R

W

ACKNOWLEDGMENTS

This book, although it has our names on the cover, is really the product of a mighty team of amazing people! First, we would like to thank Reid Tracy who pushed us to create this book. We don't usually write to a lay audience, but Reid had a vision that pushed us to make solution focused living applicable to everyone! We are indebted to Reid for having a desired outcome and helping us to catch the vision! Thank you for trusting us with this process.

We would also like to thank the whole Hay House team. We couldn't have completed this project without your support, guidance, and belief. We are showered with continual support and appreciate each of you contributing your expertise to our work! What an amazing team of people we get to work with!. A special thank you goes out to Melody Guy, our editor at Hay House. Thank you for guiding this process while allowing us to stay true to who we are. We appreciate you pushing us to make this book better and for making this happen even on the toughest days! We appreciate you.

A special thank you also goes out to Kathryn Purdie! You are masterful at what you do! Thank you for seeing each of us for who we are and for helping us to maximize our individual voices and perspectives. This book literally wouldn't have been possible without you. You are a true artist and we value your contribution more than you will ever know. We are thankful that God sent you into our lives!

Next we would like to thank the creators of solution focused brief therapy, Steve de Shazer, Insoo Kim Berg, Eve Lipchik, and others. Without their willingness to push psychotherapy to new heights, we wouldn't have huge shoulders to stand on. Thank you for your courage, your significant work, your attention to what works, and your willingness to focus on what truly matters to people. Thank you also goes out to Chris Iveson, Evan George, and Harvey Ratner. Thank you for mentoring us throughout our SFBT journey and for showing us that this approach can continue to evolve. Thank you for believing in us and valuing our contribution. We couldn't have written this book without your help and support along the way.

We would like to thank our true teacher, our many clients, who have allowed us to interact with them while trying to use solution focused brief therapy. Thank you to those who have trusted us with your most intimate stories. Thank you to each of you who have allowed us to ask you these solution focused questions and who have been willing to dig deep to find meaningful and helpful answers. Thank you for inspiring us while using your strength to change the very nature of who you are. We are honored that we have been able to walk with you along your journey in life. Thank you!

Finally, without the never-ending support and love from Becca, Rachel, Toby, Julia, and from Carmesia, Madison, and David we never could have followed our dreams and pursued this fulfilling work. Thank you for sacrificing endlessly in order to allow this book and all of our other work to come about. We know that we can hold this solution focused perspective and stance because we are surrounded with amazing people like you! Thank you and we love you!

ABOUT THE AUTHORS

Elliott Connie is an accomplished psychotherapist and a leading voice in the field of solution focused brief therapy. He's been credentialed since 2006 and been in private practice since 2008. He has a bachelor's in psychology and a master's of science in professional counseling. He has worked alongside some of the most prominent figures in the SFBT field. Additionally, Elliott has lectured all over the United States as well as internationally, in places such as the United Kingdom, Russia, India, and Australia.

Adam Froerer is one of the leading SFBT researchers and trainers. He has a bachelor's degree in psychology, a master's of education in marriage and family therapy, and a doctorate of philosophy also in marriage and family therapy. He worked as a university professor for 11 years, training marriage and family therapists and clinical psychologists. Adam has had the privilege of working with amazing clinicians, trainers, and researchers from around the globe.

Adam and Elliott founded the Solution Focused Universe (SFU), the largest solution focused training institute in the world. Through live and online courses and trainings, they train approximately 15,000 individuals annually. The SFU also houses the largest library of solution focused training material available. Because this work is so important to them, and because they want to make sure this approach gets out to the whole world, they are also behind the training institute that provides the most free content in the world.

Hay House Titles of Related Interest

YOU CAN HEAL YOUR LIFE, the movie,
starring Louise Hay & Friends
(available as an online streaming video)
www.hayhouse.com/louise-movie

THE SHIFT, the movie,
starring Dr. Wayne W. Dyer
(available as an online streaming video)
www.hayhouse.com/the-shift-movie

***

THE SOLUTION FOCUSED BRIEF THERAPY DIAMOND: A New Approach to SFBT That Will Empower Both Practitioner and Client to Achieve the Best Outcomes, by Elliott E. Connie and Adam S. Froerer

BLISS BRAIN: The Neuroscience of Remodeling Your Brain for Resilience, Creativity, and Joy
by Dawson Church, Ph.D.

BREAKING THE HABIT OF BEING YOURSELF: How to Lose Your Mind and Create a New One, by Dr. Joe Dispenza

LIMITLESS: Upgrade Your Brain, Learn Anything Faster, and Unlock Your Exceptional Life, by Jim Kwik

WHOLE BRIAN LIVING: The Anatomy of Choice and the Four Characters That Drive Our Life, by Jill Bolte Taylor

***

We hope you enjoyed this Hay House book. If you'd like to receive our online catalog featuring additional information on Hay House books and products, or if you'd like to find out more about the Hay Foundation, please contact:

HAY
HOUSE

Hay House Publishers (India) Pvt Ltd
Muskaan Complex, Plot No. 3,
B-2, Vasant Kunj, New Delhi 110 070
Phone: +91 11 41761620
www.hayhouse.co.in

—

Published in the United States by:
Hay House LLC, P.O. Box 5100, Carlsbad, CA 92018-5100
(760) 31-7695 or (800) 654-5126
www.hayhouse.com® • www.hayfoundation.org

Published in Australia by:
Hay House Australia Publishing Pty Ltd
18/36 Ralph St., Alexandria NSW 2015
Phone: +61 (02) 9669 4299
www.hayhouse.com.au

Published in the United Kingdom by:
Hay House UK Ltd
1st Floor, Crawford Corner,
91–93 Baker Street, London W1U 6QQ
Phone: +44 (0)20 3927 7290
www.hayhouse.co.uk

—

'The gateways to wisdom and knowledge are always open.'

Louise Hay